Vintage Views Along Scenic M-22 including Sleeping Bear Dunes

M. Christine Byron & Thomas R. Wilson

Vintage Views Press

Publisher's Cataloging-in-Publication Data:

Byron, M. Christine, 1949-

Vintage views along scenic M-22 including Sleeping Bear Dunes / M. Christine Byron & Thomas R. Wilson. -- First edition. -- Grand Rapids, Michigan : Vintage Views Press, [2015]

pages : illustrations ; cm.

ISBN: 978-0-9962173-0-9
Includes bibliographical references and index.

Summary: A pictorial history of Michigan's iconic road, which starts in northern Manistee County, traverses the western side of Benzie County, and loops around the Leelanau Peninsula. The book uses historical photographs, postcards, maps, and ephemera to portray the quaint towns, the beautiful lakes and stunning dunes, the old resorts, and various roadside attractions along the M-22 corridor.--Publisher.

1. Michigan Highway 22 (Mich.)--History--Pictorial works. 2. Michigan Highway 22 (Mich.)--Buildings, structures, etc.--Pictorial works.
3. Michigan--History, Local--Pictorial works. 4. Michigan--Description and travel--Pictorial works. 5. Automobile travel--Michigan--History--Pictorial works. 6. Tourism--Michigan--History--Pictorial works.
7. Roadside architecture--Michigan--History--Pictorial works.
8. Postcards--Michigan--Michigan Highway 22 (Mich.). 9. Leelanau County (Mich.)--History--Pictorial works. 10. Benzie County (Mich.)--History--Pictorial works. 11. Manistee County (Mich.)--History--Pictorial works. 12. Sleeping Bear Dunes National Lakeshore (Mich.)--History--Pictorial works. I. Wilson, Thomas R., 1949- II. Title.

F567 .B978 2015   2015936745

977.4/04--dc23   1505

First edition

Book design by Rob Burdick, Grand Rapids Michigan

Cover photo courtesy of Lake County Illinois Discovery Museum, Curt Teich Postcard Archives. Hand-colored by Dianne Carroll Burdick

Vintage Views Press
Grand Rapids, Michigan
www.vintageviewspress.com

Printed in Canada

Dedication

This book is dedicated to all the historians who work to preserve the unique history of their respective communities. Especially Kim Kelderhouse of the Leelanau Historical Society, Dave Taghon of the Empire Area Heritage Group and Dr. Louis Yock of the Benzie Area Historical Society - you have all been such a great help to us with our research and endless questions. Your knowledge, skills and dedication are truly amazing!

Acknowledgements

SCENE ON HIGHWAY 22 PORTAGE LAKE ONEKAMA MICH.
3384

For their time, knowledge, and generous resources, we wish to thank all the people and institutions that helped us with this book.

Several institutions gave us permission to use materials from their collections. Thanks to the Arcadia Area Historical Museum and Lyle Matteson & Joyce Howard; Archives of Michigan and Jessica Harden; Bentley Historical Society and Karen Jania; Benzie Area Historical Society and Dr. Louis Yock, Nancy Norton-Taylor & Andy Bolange; Curt Teich Postcard Archives and Heather Johnson; the Empire Heritage Group and Dave Taghon; Grand Rapids Public Library and Tim Gleisner & Melissa Fox; Grand Rapids Public Museum and Alex Forist & Andrea Melvin; Great Lakes Commission and Christine Manninen; Leelanau Historical Society and Kim Kelderhouse; Leelanau School Archives and Joe Blondia; the Northport Area Heritage Group and Sue Hanson, Martha Roberts, & Al Noftz; Omena Historical Society and Joey Bensley & Marsha Buehler; MLive Media Group and Michael D. Gillis; Michigan State University Archives and Megan Malone; Sleeping Bear Dunes National Lakeshore and Laura Quackenbush & Kim Mann; Networks Northwest and Sarah Lucas; Traverse City District Library and Katheryn Carrier; Traverse City History Center and Peg Siciliano & Dave Pennington; and last but not least, the West Michigan Tourist Association and Rick Hert.

Special thanks to the Michigan Department of Transportation (MDOT) and Kim Henderson & Gary Eiseler for use of the M-22 signage logo.

We are thankful to the businesses that shared images with us: Art's Tavern and Tim Barr & Bonnie Nesco; Camp Tosebo and Dave Wallace; Chimney Corners and Mary Rogers; Fischer's Happy Hour Tavern and Paul Fischer; Leland Mercantile and Joe Burda.

Many thanks to the fellow postcard collectors who shared their personal collections with us: Judith Anderson, Jill Cheney, Lynn Contos, Lyle Matteson, and Grace and Steve Truman.

Phil Balyeat, a legendary photographer of northern Michigan, allowed us to use several of his wonderful photographs in the book.

Michael Huey contributed his knowledge of Camp Leelanau for Boys, Camp Kohahna, and the Leelanau Schools, and the Homestead, as well as photographs from the Witt-Dorring Family Archives. Karl Bahle shared postcards from the Owen Bahle Collection. Many thanks to both of them for sharing their family's history.

Other individuals who offered their advice and encouragement include postcard dealers Doug Aikenhead, Don Harrison, and Wally Jung. And for their unfailing support in our work, we thank George Weeks and Tom Dilley.

We also wish to thank Alan Campbell of the *Leelanau Enterprise* for use of vintage advertisements and graphicsf. The *Leelanau Enterprise* has made a substantial contribution to the history of the county with its weekly articles of historical interest. The newspaper is a primary source of information for researchers and historians.

For legal advice on copyright issues and his interest in history, we thank James A. Mitchell.

We give great thanks to Rob Burdick for designing the book and for his patience and understanding in dealing with all the details it takes to put a book like this together. Dianne Carroll Burdick beautifully hand-colored the photograph on the cover. Many thanks to Dianna Stampfler for writing the Foreword, there isn't a person more interested in promoting Michigan than Dianna. We whole-heartedly thank Marcie Beck for proofing our manuscript and making relevant corrections and suggestions. And many thanks to Tom Vranich from Friesens printers for his guidance in publishing this book.

Foreword

I like to think I have a pretty good cache of historical tidbits about Michigan. And yet every time I flip through the pages of one of Chris and Tom's books, or sit down to have casual discussions with them about our statewide travels, I discover new treasures to add to my trove. Having a sneak peak at *Vintage Views Along Scenic M-22* was as much an honor as the request to write this Foreword.

My first introduction to these inspiring collectors and authors was before their first *Vintage Views* book was even published, while I was working at the West Michigan Tourist Association and Chris was working in the Michigan History Room at the Grand Rapids Public Library. There was a natural connection and mutual fascination with Michigan's early travel history and the marketing materials that were used to promote the various resorts, routes and communities—specifically along the Great Lakes shorelines.

Promoting M-22 isn't a new concept. Since the early 1900s, tourism organizations have been touting this scenic 116-mile, three-county route for its year-round natural resources, quaint coastal towns and unparalleled vistas (which ironically haven't changed much in the past 80 years).

Advertisements boast of white sand beaches, fragrant orchards and pure drinking water from artesian wells. Handwritten postcards—a lost art—give a glimpse at the day-in-the-life of vacationers and their love of the area.

Resort brochures offer seasonal rates of $200 (which today is often the nightly rate at the high end resorts along the route). While a handful of historic resorts, like Chimney Corners and Portage Point Inn, still welcome guests, others such as the Sleeping Bear Inn and Ken-Tuck-U-Inn have long since closed their doors.

Also lost to time are the days of sand skiing, dunesmobiles, and horseback riding along the shoreline. Yet, glider rides—which saw their heyday soar in the 1930s from the towering sand dune areas—are still offered in Frankfort during the summer season.

Youth and church retreat facilities, artist colonies, and private clubs were prevalent in this area, providing members with the best in modern amenities and locales for rest, relaxation and recreation. Even today, the M-22 corridor is a haven for creative types, entrepreneurs and those seeking a slower paced lifestyle.

Flipping through the pages of *Vintage Views Along Scenic M-22* is literally an historical journey through time, before cell phones and social media. Each photo, caption, and narrative evoke a longing to step inside the page and experience these captured moments firsthand: to sit on the porch of the Blue Lantern Tea Room on a sunny afternoon, take in a round of golf at Crystal Downs, walk through Lund's Scenic Garden or purchase moccasins at the Indian Craft Shop.

It has been through the *Vintage Views* series, and a growing friendship with Chris and Tom, that I have started my own collection of Michigan postcards, souvenirs, collectibles, posters and other mementoes to decorate my home. Of course, autographed copies of each of their books are prominently featured in my collection and this M-22 edition is sure to be one of my most treasured titles.

Dianna Stampfler
President, Promote Michigan

M22 Leland Mich - 35

Preface

With this, our fifth book, we have turned to scenic M-22, our favorite road in the great state of Michigan. We know and love this route very well and drive it many times each year. We intend to give an overview of the history of the road and take readers on a "road trip" from Onekama north to Frankfort and Northport, and then south to Greilickville, outside of Traverse City. We'll stop at the towns and villages along the road and visit old inns, resorts, souvenir shops, and other interesting spots. We'll stop for gas in Empire and tea in Leland. Roadside attractions such as Lund's Scenic Garden and Glen Magic will beckon us to stop. We'll explore the majesty of Sleeping Bear Dunes and take a dunesmobile ride over "Michigan's Sahara." Maybe we'll land a catch at Raff's Fishing Camp or at the Good Harbor Trout Preserve, or watch more skilled fishermen bring in their catch at Fishtown. Summer camps will keep us busy with hiking, canoeing and horseback riding. We'll visit lighthouses and life saving stations and learn about their role in keeping safe the maritime traffic on Lake Michigan. We'll visit state parks and learn how Sleeping Bear Dunes became a National Lakeshore.

Using postcards, photographs, maps, and advertisements, we have tried to evoke a kind of time-travel to an earlier time and place. We have used quotations from old tourist ephemera, newspapers and magazines that described a scene or gave a taste of what it was like to be there at the time. We have eavesdropped on postcard messages sent from vacation spots to friends and family back home. In quoting these writings and messages, we have kept the original misspellings, incorrect grammar, inaccuracies, and exaggerations. We have tried to give some background on the various towns and villages and their hotels, resorts, camps and shops to the best of our ability. Information on some of the places was sketchy. As with our other four books, we have attempted to give a flavor of the past, not to document it in a dry, scholarly style.

We have drawn extensively from our personal collection of postcards and tourist ephemera, but could not have done the book without help from various museums, historical societies, archives and libraries. We have the good fortune to know a number of postcard collectors who were willing to share their treasures with us. We have acknowledged the sources of images used in a list at the end of the book.

We invite you to take a road trip with us on scenic M-22 and hope you enjoy the ride. Don't forget to send a postcard to the folks back home.

Table of Contents

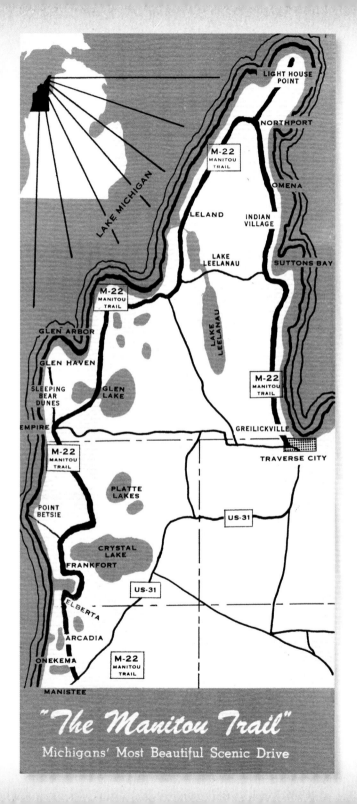

This photo shows Rhoda Wheeler's auto being pulled out of the mud by a farmer's horses in 1905. Ms. Wheeler was on her way to visit her aunt and uncle, owners of the Sunset Lodge in Omena.

Chapter One

The History of M-22

The history of the M-22 route goes back to the times when Native Americans lived along Lake Michigan's shores. The earliest "roads" were Native American footpaths. A section of the M-22 route was once an Indian trail running from Leland along the shore of Lake Michigan for a few miles, then cutting inland toward Northport, then running south along the shore of Grand Traverse Bay to Omena and Suttons Bay. While the original M-22 route cut inland from Suttons Bay to Traverse City, the old Indian trail along the bay more closely followed the route of M-22 today.

The earliest road into northern Michigan was the Newago and Northport State Road. An act of the Michigan legislature approved the construction of the road in 1859. The route was laid out by Perry Hannah of Traverse City, who at the time was a member of the State Road Commission. The Newago Northport road ran from Newago to Traverse City, then continuing north, it ran along the west shore of Grand Traverse Bay to Omena. It then moved inland to Northport, much as the current route of M-22 does today. At times the road followed the old Indian trail. Until this road was completed about 1863, people arrived in Leelanau County by boat. The road brought more settlers into the region and connected them to their neighbors as horse and buggy travel took hold. As farming communities became established, farm to market roads were built, but they usually only serviced an area of six to ten miles.

The automobile brought major changes to travel. With an increase in auto sales came the need for better roads. But surprisingly, the first call for better roads came from the bicycling craze of the 1880s. Bicyclists faced dangerous conditions on the old rutted wagon roads and crusaded for better roads, starting the Good Roads movement. Soon automobilists joined the campaign and the cry for better roads was heard far and wide. The Michigan State Highway Department was established in 1905 with Horatio "Good Roads" Earle as its first commissioner.

Wagons still outnumbered autos in the first decade of the 20th century. David H. Day of Glen Haven was one of the few people in Leelanau County who owned an automobile. An early promoter of good roads, Day's first auto was a Peerless touring car. In 1910 he purchased a new Model 17 Buick which was delivered to the Buick garage in Traverse City. The roads at the time were pretty bad, in some places little more than sand trails or mud. The few autos on these poor roads often became stuck in wagon ruts or mired in mud. Mechanical breakdowns and flat tires were frequent. Horseshoe nails were the most common cause of flat tires. With garages few and far between, early motorists had to be prepared to handle breakdowns and repairs on their own. A trip that today might take only a few hours, would have taken days.

In 1913 state funds became available to townships and counties for roads built to meet specific criteria. These roads were known as State Reward Roads. Grass roots organizations, like the West Michigan Pike Association, were formed to promote specific routes, such as the West Michigan Pike, which evolved into US-31. Reacting to the interests of these grass roots organizations, in 1913 the State enacted the State Reward Trunk Line Highways Act, which established routes from point to point, leaving the local governmental units to lay out the specific roads. A scenic loop of the West Michigan Pike, which later became M-22, was designated to run from "Manistee through Arcadia, Frankfort, Empire, Glen Haven, Leland, Northport, Omena, Suttons Bay to Traverse City." This route became known as "going round the horn."

West Michigan Pike Association
(West Michigan Lake Shore Highway Association)

The above 1913 photo shows members of West Michigan Lake Shore Highway Association in front of the old Park Place Hotel in Traverse City.

This photo shows D.H. Day, on the far right, stopping in Empire on one of the Pike tours circa 1915.

The scenic M-22 route had its beginnings in the work of the West Michigan Lake Shore Highway Association, which was formed on January 10, 1913. Recognizing the need for a continuous road up the west coast of Michigan, a meeting was organized in Muskegon and representatives from all the lakeshore counties attended. In May of 1913 the lengthy name of the consortium was changed to the shorter West Michigan Pike Association. The organizers patched together a route from Michigan City to Mackinaw City, which became known as the West Michigan Pike. Most of that route is now US-31. From the beginning there were two scenic loops of the Pike, the roads that are now M-22 and M-119.

The M-22 route began in northern Manistee County, traversed the western side of Benzie County and looped around the Leelanau Peninsula. It was largely through the efforts of D.H. Day that the M-22 route was chosen as an official loop of the highway. Day was known throughout western Michigan as a good roads booster. As president of the Western Michigan Development Bureau, Day often stressed the importance of good roads for the benefit of agriculture, industry and tourism.

For several years between 1913 and 1922, the West Michigan Pike Association staged auto tours along the Pike route. D.H. Day often hosted luncheons for the "pikers" at his farm in Glen Haven. As the *Grand Rapids Progress* in August 1915 reported:

"Mr. Day's hospitality will not soon be forgotten, neither will his beautiful home and surroundings. On the shores of Lake Michigan in Glen Arbor Township, Leelanau County, is the home of one of the greatest Good Roads boosters in all Michigan. Mr. Day's contribution in time and money to the West Michigan Pike Association will perhaps not be fully appreciated and understood during the present generation, except by those who know him best and have recognized the value of his contributions."

In 2001 M-109 was designated as the D.H. Day Highway, giving long-overdue recognition to the efforts of this early good roads promoter.

**Five Miles North of Manistee,
the West Michigan Pike Splits into the Main Route and the Scenic Route at the "Parting of the Ways."
The Scenic Tour "Around the Horn" Begins.**

"Five miles from the 'Parting of the Ways,' the Pike emerges from the hills on the south side of Portage Lake and circles the eastern end for three miles into the village of O-nek-ema (Indian word signifying 'Place of Great Beauty'). The village lies at the base of a great hill, and by many is considered the most beautiful point on the whole Pike route. It is famous for its artesian and natural gas wells and its harbor of refuge is one of the finest on the Great Lakes.

Frankfort is the largest city in Benzie County, and is its commercial center. It is well known because of its flowing mineral springs, one of which pours forth waters with a sulphur base, and the other water strongly impregnated with iron. These waters have an excellent tonic quality, and were frequented by the Indians before the arrival of the white man.

A mile and a half north is Crystal Lake, one of the most charming lakes of Michigan, with a dozen well-known resorts.

For beauty of scenery, Glen Lake is classed as the equal of Lake George, and by some even of Lake Como. It is a body of clear water, surrounded by hills. The lake bottom is sand, thru which bubbles water that keeps the lake at the point of overflowing. The lake is from one to three miles wide, and seven miles long.

The points of interest about the lake are the Sleeping Bear on the west, the big private forest belonging to D.H. Day on the north, the winding river which carries the surplus water into Sleeping Bear Bay, and the high range of hills bordering the lake on the east, which hills are fast being taken for orchard propositions.

The Sleeping Bear is of interest because of its wonderful formation and its historic associations. It is a sand dune five miles long and from one to one and a half miles wide. Its highest point is 490 feet above the level of Lake Michigan. From its top may be watched the big steamers that are constantly passing up and down Lake Michigan.

Northport is beautifully located on a series of terraces rising from the shores of Northport Bay, and is the most important cherry shipping center of northwestern Michigan. Numerous cherry orchards have been set out in the past ten years and have just come into bearing. The Dame orchard, with 16,000 cherry trees of the Montmorency variety alone, ranks as the largest orchard in the world.

Peshawbetown is an Indian village near Omena, and is interesting material for ethnological study. Here are real Indians living according to their own inclinations. Aghosatown, just north of Omena, has a similar population."

-Scarborough's Official Tour Book, 1916

3

Driving Directions

Before road maps were a common item in every car's glove box, travelers had to rely on incomplete or confusing signage marking the roads. Detailed driving directions given in various guide books were welcomed by motorists. The West Michigan Pike Association published annual guides for several years. There were also national guide books such as the *Official Automobile Blue Book, Scarborough's Official Tour Book* and *King's Official Route Guide*. These thick volumes gave route directions with mileage from town to town, similar to Mapquest of today.

"Manistee to Onekama, Arcadia, Elberta and Frankfort
35 Miles

0.0	**Manistee** at Division and River Sts. Go east on River St. to
0.1	Smith St. Turn sharp left across bridge over Manistee River, bearing right at fork into Cleveland St. Pick up trolley. Follow trolley out of city, bearing right with trolley at fork. (Orchard Beach Road to left.)
5.1	'Parting of the Way.' Orchards on each side. Two signboards. Bear left.
8.0	Turn right with travel on winding road to
10.0	End of road. Portage Lake ahead. Turn left, circling Lake into village.
12.6	**Onekama**. Straight ahead along shore to
13.3	Fork. Bear right up hill. (This hill is one mile long. Beautiful scenery, especially from top of bank at the left of the crest of this hill.) Follow main travel, jogging right and left at 17.6.
18.6	Four corners. Turn left.
19.0	End of road. Turn right, following winding road. Caution for steep down grade thru woods. Cross head of Bar Lake to outskirts of
22.2	**Arcadia**. Village to left. Turn right.
23.0	Left-hand road toward woods. Turn left, going up grade thru woods. Winding road. Follow main travel northward (Benzie County). Beautiful view of Herring Lakes and Lake Michigan. Caution for steep down grade. Follow main travel north across Herring Lake valley and up grade 29.8. View of Betsey River valley. At foot of long hill, road ends.
31.5	School on left. Turn left, angling right with road into
33.0	**Elberta**. Business section. Turn right across railroad and bridge over Betsey River. Bear left at fork, crossing railroad. (Road at right leads to Benzonia.) Continue along shore of lake, turning left and go straight.
35.0	**Frankfort**. Center of City.

Frankfort to Empire, Glen Haven, Leland, Northport, Omena, Suttons Bay and Traverse City
88.0 miles

0.0	**Leave Frankfort** at Main and Seventh Sts. Go north on Seventh St. 3 blocks, angling left at fork. Church on right. Follow main travel around numerous turns, coming out on shore of Crystal Lake. Thru Crystalia. Bear left around lake to
4.4	Fork. Bear left away from lake. Follow winding road thru woods, avoiding all crossroads. Cross Platte River 12.0. Bear left 14.8, avoiding sandhill, to
15.3	Right-hand road. Turn right one-half mile to
15.8	Four corners. Turn left and go north 4 miles, passing school on left 19.8. Just beyond, angle left. Thru woods and down steep hill into village of
21.4	**Empire**. Turn right around stores and at watering trough turn left with travel. Bear right up hill just beyond.
23.7	Fork. Bear left, passing cemetery. Thru three corners. Curve left and right thru woods around west end of Glen Lake. McIntyre hill 25.1. Fine view over lake. Cross railroad 27.3. Sawmill on left. Up grade past Day farm to crest of hill overlooking Sleeping Bear Bay. Bear right and left down grade to
28.3	**Glen Haven**. Pier and stores ahead. Turn right, going straight thru.
30.4	**Glen Arbor**. Cross Crystal River at grist mill 31.3.
32.6	Bear right. Bear right 33.9 to
34.5	Four corners. Bear right with travel. Pass small lake on left 36.0. Bass Lake on right 37.5. Swing left, passing Traverse Lake. Sugar Loaf Mt. on right. Thru Good Harbor 42.7. Bear left at fork 43.1. Bear left at three corners 46.5, passing school on right. Along shore of Lake Leelanau (to right), across bridge into
48.7	**Leland**. Hotel on right. Straight thru. Pass cemetery on right 50.2. Bear right around head of lake. Keep left 51.9. Turn right 56.7. Turn left 58.4. Thru cut down grade into outskirts of
59.7	**Northport**. Turn right. Cross bridge 61.6. Bear left at fork 62.7. Grand Traverse Bay to left. Pass Aghosatown. Turn right across bridge into village of
64.7	**Omena**. Postoffice on right. Keep left along shore. Pass hotel. Cross railroad 66.4. Thru Peshawbatown 67.8. Cross railroad 69.5 and 70.9. Bear left into village of
71.2	**Suttons Bay**. Bear left across railroad 71.8. Bear right 72.6. Turn right with travel 75.9, with West Arm of Bay on left. Keep to left along Bay shore. Pass Greilickville. Into outskirts of city just beyond factory 87.3. Turn right on Maple St. At Front St. 87.5 turn left.
88.0	**Traverse City**. Front and Union Sts."

-Scarborough's Official Tour Book, 1916

Signage on M-22

Before M-22 had a number, it had a name as part of the West Michigan Pike. This was a common tradition at a time when there weren't many roads. Michigan was the second state, following Wisconsin, to identify highways by numbers, giving each trunkline a "M" designation. The West Michigan Pike became M-11, and the scenic loop "Around the Horn" became M-22. The numbered designations were created about 1918-1919, but didn't start appearing on road maps until about 1920. Posting the signs on the roads was completed sometime in 1921.

The first "West Michigan Pike" signs were created in 1914. The metal signs were intended to be posted in conspicuous places along the road and at corners to indicate turns. Later concrete posts marked the Pike, but these were located mostly on the southern portion of the highway.

The earliest trunkline signs used an elongated diamond with a block letter "M" at the top, the words "State Trunkline" in the middle, and the specific road number below. They could either be securely wrapped around a utility pole or independently mounted on stand-alone posts.

In 1926 the diamond-shaped sign was redesigned with 90 degree angles, and the road number was given in a black font on a white background. In 1948 when the U.S. Highway route signs were changed to use the federally prescribed typeface, Michigan's trunkline signs followed suit - changing the font of the numerals, but keeping the block "M."

In 1971 the Federal Highway Administration mandated specifications that black "sign blanks" be used as a background for traffic signage. Michigan's standard diamond shape was incorporated into a black square as it appears today. For more than three decades these signs have stayed relatively unchanged.

These photos show the State Reward Road, M-22, in Bingham Township being graded using horse-drawn drag scoops. This original route of M-22 on the east side of the Leelanau Peninsula was the road we know today as C-633, or Center Highway.

Building M-22

In the early 1900s there were no paved roads in the Grand Traverse region. Roads were nothing more than dirt wagon paths or sand trails, little wider than a two-track. Road building was the responsibility of townships until 1905 when legislation gave voters the power to establish county road commissions. While Manistee and Leelanau Counties approved county control of road building early on, Benzie County did not establish a county road commission until 1930.

The route that became M-22 did not always follow the current roadway. Some portions were significantly rerouted to provide a more direct or more scenic route. Other segments were altered to avoid dangerous turns. While improvements were being made on M-22, there were often long detours.

Some segments of M-22 in Manistee and Benzie Counties were improved and straightened. A short segment of new M-22 was constructed to straighten the road from Arcadia north to the Manistee-Benzie County line. In 1939 workers for the W.P.A. began that work, but construction was not completed until 1942.

M-22 followed the road we now know as M-109 until 1922, when it was realigned from the southern end of M-109 to Glen Arbor, crossing the Narrows at Glen Lake. The route of M-109, which at the time was not a state trunkline, was turned back to local control. Then about 1929, it became a state highway and was given the designation M-109.

M-22 on the east side of Leelanau County was originally located inland from Grand Traverse Bay, following what is known today as C-633 (Cherry Bend Road and Center Highway), from Greilickville to Suttons Bay. Starting in 1936, approximately three miles of M-22 were relocated along the shore of the West Arm of the bay from Greilickville to Crain Hill Road, then west to Center Highway. In 1949 the remaining segment of M-22 was realigned from its previous course on Center Highway, to complete the shoreline route to Suttons Bay.

By the end of the 1920s most of M-22 was improved to hard surface or gravel. "Hard surface" roads referred to roads merely graded to remove loose soil or sand to provide a uniform hard surface. The better "gravel roads" were graded with a crown for water runoff, then a clay base was laid on the road with a top layer of gravel. While road conditions improved on main highways such as US-31, secondary highways like M-22, remained mostly gravel into the 1930s, with only small sections actually paved.

As automobile traffic expanded on M-22, so did the wear and tear on the road. Gravel could not support the increased automobile use. The growing demand for maintenance provided economic incentive for paving the road with concrete or asphalt. These surfaces cost less to maintain and provided a better driving experience.

M-22 was gradually paved in sections. "Paved road" could be either asphalt or concrete. In 1928 one of the first sections to be paved with concrete was completed through the village of Leland. By 1942, M-22 had been paved through Manistee and Benzie Counties, and most of Leelanau County, except for the stretch between Leland and Northport, which was not paved until 1946. The section of M-22 from Suttons Bay to Greilickville was paved as part of the work on road realignment. This work started in 1936 was completed in 1949.

These photos show concrete being mixed on site, poured into forms and leveled in front of the old Harbor House building on Main Street in Leland. By the end of September 1928, M-22 was paved with concrete from the Duck Lake corner through the village.

M-22 Associations

Over the years four separate associations were formed to promote scenic M-22. The first "M-22 Association" was formed in November of 1929. The *Leelanau Enterprise* stated in its November 14th issue, "Believing that united efforts will produce results in the improvement of the M-22 highway, the four counties, Leelanau, Grand Traverse, Benzie and Manistee will join in an association for that purpose." The first M-22 Association met in Leland. The group felt that highway improvements in other sections of Michigan were receiving much more attention and that its region should campaign for its share. For months the Association sought a name for M-22 that would capture the public's attention. An appropriate name, the "Chippewa Trail," was chosen on February 25, 1930 while the Association was meeting in the Chippewa Hotel in Manistee. A logo with an Indian head was selected for the route, but plans to print 25,000 promotional brochures were abandoned as the Great Depression took hold and funding for road improvements dried up. Although the name "Chippewa Trial" never fell into popular usage, the group did attain some publicity in attracting travelers to M-22.

The second association promoting M-22 was founded in May of 1940 when Leelanau County organized the "Traverse City to Northport M-22 Highway Association." Its purpose was to work for the completion of a hard surfaced road long the bay shore from Traverse City to Northport. Some progress was made on paving this section of road, but with WWII intervening, this work was not completed until 1949.

A third "M-22 Association" was formed in February of 1953. Allen Blacklock, Mayor of Elberta, and the Elberta Chamber of Commerce invited all the municipalities along M-22 to unite in an effort to draw tourists and travelers off US-31 outside of Manistee and onto M-22. Funds were solicited from the towns and cities, as well as businesses along the road. About 15,000 M-22 brochures were produced and distributed. A large sign was erected just south of the US-31/M-22 intersection. Newspaper publicity also brought attention to the scenic M-22 route and points of interest on the road.

The fourth association promoting M-22 had roots in the "Michigamme Trail Association," which was organized in the early 1960s by the Pentwater Chamber of Commerce. Under the leadership of Herbert Behr, the group began promoting the idea of a scenic route to lure tourists off the state's freeways and instead to travel leisurely along scenic roads closer to the Lake Michigan shore. The name "Michigamme Trail" was chosen for the proposed route, which followed the length of Lake Michigan's shoreline through 14 Michigan counties. "Michigamme" is an Indian word meaning "big water" and signs were designed that showed a Native American in full headdress on the left, with the name of the route on the right. However, the State Highway Department would not approve the signs because of federal guidelines prohibiting non-conforming signs along national highways. Since segments of US-12 and US-31 were part of the proposed route, the planned signage was abandoned. The organization also dropped plans to print 50,000 strip maps of the route and the coalition faded away. But a separate group picked up the banner about 1965 and formed the "M-22 Association of the Michigamme Trail," and publicized the attractions of M-22 through brochures and advertisements in tourist guides.

Concrete Roads

With the formation of the first M-22 Association in 1929, there was a push to pave all of M-22. Hugh J. Gray of the West Michigan Tourist and Resort Association proclaimed that "tourists want pavement." When the tourist association published its 1930 maps of Benzie and Leelanau Counties, it was noted that "M-22 is an excellent gravel road the entire distance through [Benzie] County." The same was said of Leelanau County, "except for a short stretch, which is good county road, between Leland and Northport." See pages 39 and 77 in this book for these maps.

In 1930, one year after the first association was formed to promote scenic M-22, the Frankfort gateway sign was changed to read "Scenic M-22 Road." Undoubtedly, this was the work of influential members of the association.

M-22 - Most Scenery per Mile

"Land and water and sky spread out in a magnificence of panorama and grandeur of spectacle - these characterize M-22 throughout its 119 miles, up along the coast of Michigan and around the Leelanau Peninsula.

Most scenery per mile is the claim that is made for it, and you will agree, after you have traversed it, that only superlative phrases will do it justice."

-Michigan Scenic Highways: Around Lake Michigan Tour, 1933

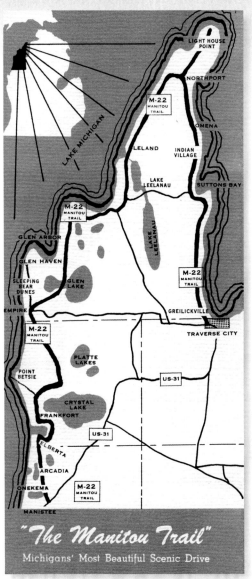

M-22 - "The Manitou Trail"

The third M-22 Association, formed to promote tourism and travel along the road, was established in 1953. The Association had plans to extensively publicize the route's attractions and wanted a memorable name to use in promotion. Owen Bahle of Suttons Bay was the publicity chairman of the group, and he proposed that the Association sponsor a contest to give a name to the M-22 route. More than 500 entries were submitted. There were several entries suggesting the name, "The Manitou Trail." The earliest entry for that name was chosen, and William H. Nash, a native of Leelanau County, won a prize of $10.00. The Association published a brochure, "M-22 - The Manitou Trail," which listed points of interest including Sleeping Bear Sand Dunes, Lund's Scenic Gardens, a Platte River boat trip, the Indian village of Peshawbestown, color tours and winter sports. It also highlighted the eleven villages along the way.

Not a Short Cut

"The Manitou Trail, a leisurely traveled highway thru some of Michigan's most beautiful scenery, is not a short cut. It is reserved for those who desire a scenic drive over uncrowded highways thru a countryside cooled by lake breezes."

-M-22 "The Manitou Trail," circa 1955

The M-22 Association published advertisements promoting "The Manitou Trail." The ad shown below was published in *Benzie County Vacationland*, circa 1955. The ad on the right was published in the West Michigan Tourist Association's *Carefree Days in West Michigan* in 1958.

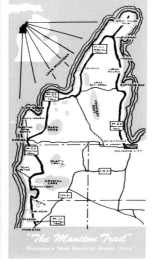

M-22...

"The Manitou Trail"

One of America's Famous Scenic Routes

PLEASANT MOTORING over an uncrowded highway, through Michigan's most magnificent country along Lake Michigan and around the Leelanau Peninsula. A ride that will be the delight of your vacation travels. Places of interest, activities, superb dining and excellent accommodations at the many communities and resort centers along the way.

AN IDEAL TRIP ON YOUR TOUR TO THE MACKINAC BRIDGE

Frequent turnouts are provided so you may fully enjoy the grandeur of every vista. Points of interest include beautiful Glen Lake and Lake Leelanau, spacious beaches along Lake Michigan and crystal-clear inland waters; the world-renowned Sleeping Bear sand dunes; health giving artesian wells; carferry fleet, lumber mills, quaint fishing village, scenic gardens, river boat trips, Indian village and many other sights. Along the way are these communities;

- MANISTEE • ONEKAMA • ARCADIA • ELBERTA
- FRANKFORT • EMPIRE • GLEN ARBOR • GLEN HAVEN
- LELAND • NORTHPORT • OMENA • SUTTONS BAY
- PESHAWBESTOWN • GREILICKVILLE • TRAVERSE CITY

For detailed information, brochures or reservations write the chambers of commerce in these communities or the M-22 Association, Frankfort, Michigan

---

M-22

"The Manitou Trail"

Michigans' Most Beautiful Scenic Drive

ONEKEMA — Portage Lake leads in scenic beauty seven miles from the beginning of M-22. It is noted for its health giving artesian wells, year round fishing and clear white sand beaches safe for children. Vacationers throughout the midwest have found Onekema, Portage Lake the ideal spot for relaxation and rest at one of the many Hotels, Cabins or Cottages.

ARCADIA — Village and Lake situated between green hills and along the sandy shores of Lake Michigan. Lake Arcadia is a favorite among fishermen for it produces record catches of Black Bass, Northern Pike, Musky and Pan Fish. Nearby are some of the finest and most beautiful Trout Streams for the Fly enthusiast. Cabins, Camping, Cottages and Boats are available.

ELBERTA — The public beach on Lake Michigan is one of the finest to be found anywhere. The bluffs overlooking Lake Michigan are a scenic wonderland for the amateur photographer and the finest Glider area in Michigan. The largest Ski-Jump in the State and open slope tobogganing are available to the winter sportsman. Home Port of the Ann Arbor Carferry Fleet.

FRANKFORT — The City of Frankfort offers to the Vacationer all the rest and relaxation with every type of sport that can be imagined. Swimming, fishing, boating, golf, tennis and shuffleboard are available. Hay-fever sufferers find the cool, washed air off the Lake for their relief and comfort.

EMPIRE — At the gateway to Leelanau County, a town of charm lying at the base of the Empire Bluffs. The site of extensive lumbering in by-gone days, Empire now boasts of her Cherry Orchards and rolling farmlands. North and South Bar lakes for fishing and Lake Michigan surf bathing with pleasant living accomodations nearby make this section one to visit.

GLEN LAKE — The beautiful Glen Lake Area is world famous for its brilliant blue water, its forested hills and the Sleeping Bear Sand Dunes. This is the largest traveling Dune in the Middle west and challenges the city weary vacationer with its desert-like fascination and magnificent view of Lake Michigan with Manitou and Fox Islands in the distance.

GLEN ARBOR — Heart of the old lumbering operations is one of the centers of Glen Lake activity. Scenically situated under towering pines between Lake Michigan and Glen Lake. Glen Arbor is one of the most beautiful Villages in Leelanau County.

LELAND — An average beautiful Leelanau County village, unsurpassed for scenery, lakes and climate. Swimming in crystal clear Lake Michigan or in warmer Lake Leelanau. Rating "the finest" and the best small mouth bass lake in Michigan. M.S.C. Art Colony located nearby.

NORTHPORT — A community wrapped in interesting tradition . . . of the sea . . . of Indian Lore . . . pioneer missionaries and rugged farmers wrested their land from the hardwood forests. A trip to the tip of the little finger is a must for every tourist who would enjoy the beauties of this peninsula.

OMENA — Nestles at the foot of it's own protected bay. The community was founded over 100 years ago as a Presbyterian Mission for the Indians and the original Church is still in use. The bell of this church was cast from the old-time copper pennies that were contributed by the Indian Converts.

SUTTONS BAY — Nestling at the foot of a range of high hills, has a veritable Alpine setting. It is well known for it's excellent boat harbor and fine sand beaches. It boasts two public parks, one including a municipal bathing beach.

SCENIC DRIVE M-22 MICH. 2-394

The last segment of M-22 to be paved was completed in 1949 on the stretch between Crain Hill Road and the village of Suttons Bay. On hand for the September 9th dedication were state highway officials and other dignitaries. Shown at the microphone is Brigadier General George Schulgen of Traverse City.

M-22 Dedication

"Friday was a big day in the history of Suttons Bay, and a Ziegler Day was declared, to carry out the program for the dedication of the new M-22 to the public. The ceremonies were staged on a platform where the new highway intersects Broadway and St. Joseph Sts., Mr. Conrad A. Gronseth was master of ceremonies and introduced the various distinguished guests and speakers. State Highway Commissioner Charles M. Ziegler made a fine address and performed the ceremony of cutting the ribbon, which officially opened the new highway....

We are proud of the new highway - it makes a shorter and more convenient road to Traverse City, and it sure is a scenic drive. It is named South Shore Drive, and people traveling over the new road will have an opportunity to see the natural beauty of Leelanau County, the 'Land of Delight', as soon as they cross the county line in Traverse City, and as they progress on their journey, beautiful vistas will present themselves, and they will take back fond memories of their visit.... The new highway has no hills to negotiate, and the few curves it has are graded for speed, and the concrete adds much to comfort."

-Suttons Bay Courier, September 15, 1949

The M-22 Michigamme Trail

In the mid-1960s the M-22 Association of the Michigamme Trail published a brochure attempting to entice tired travelers to get off the expressway and see "some of the most beautiful scenery in the western hemisphere" at a leisurely pace on the M-22 section of the Michigamme Trail - the "Main Line" to Sleeping Bear Dunes. The association also published the advertisement on the right in the West Michigan Tourist Association's 1966 edition of *Carefree Days in West Michigan*.

What M-22 Offers

"The M-22 Scenic Highway skirts the finest white sand beaches to be found anywhere on Lake Michigan. Both secluded beaches and well-populated ones await the bather and picnic enthusiast.

Thousands of miles of streams and uncounted lakes in the M-22 section of Michigan give anglers some of the finest fishing in the state.... Winter and summer fishing give the angler a wide choice of fish - Bass, Walleye, Great Northern, Brookies, Brown Trout, Lake Trout, Rainbow, Whitefish, Smelt.

A wealth of unposted state and national lands gives the bow and arrow hunter and the firearms hunter a paradise to pursue his favorite game in.

You are only a few minutes drive from any spot on M-22 to some of the finest ski resorts on the midwest."

-Follow the M-22 Portion of the Michigamee Trail, circa 1966

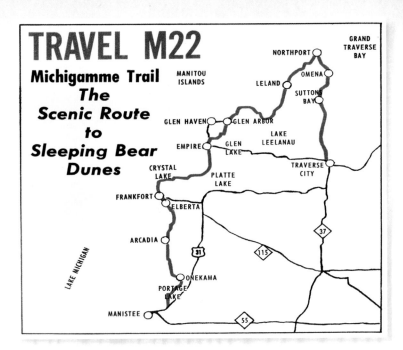

45th Parallel

The 45th parallel of latitude, also known as the Polar-Equator, crosses Leelanau County from the South Manitou lighthouse, across Lake Michigan to a spot near Leland, then across the county to a spot just a little north of the village of Suttons Bay. This means that the county is half-way between the North Pole and the Equator. This photo from 1959, shows members of the Leelanau Historical Society at the dedication of the original 45th parallel sign north of Suttons Bay. Included in the photo are Emelia Schaub (second from right), Albert Wrisley (far left), and Marion Yoder (far right). The spot for the sign was chosen by P.J. O'Non, a surveyor who calculated the point as accurately as possible. But in the days before GPS, O'Non did comment that the spot could be off a few feet one way or the other. This original sign was stolen. MDOT later placed new signs on each side of the Leelanau Peninsula, reading "45th Parallel - Halfway Between Equator and North Pole."

Several businesses in Leelanau County have taken the 45th parallel as part of their names including a vineyard, pet service, cafe and candy store. There is also Suttons Bay Township's 45th Parallel Park just north of the village of Suttons Bay. The 45th Parallel Polka Band entertains people in the region on both sides of the Polar-Equator.

Lake Michigan Circle Tour

Vacationers have been driving around Lake Michigan for years, sometimes on their own, other times as part of a motoring tour promoted by a newspaper, or on a road rally sponsored by one of the automobile clubs. In 1933 a booklet was published, *Michigan's Scenic Highways, Parks and Points of Interest - Around Lake Michigan Tour - World's Fair Edition.* The idea behind the booklet was to welcome people to Michigan who had visited the Century of Progress Exposition in Chicago and guide them to attractions along Michigan's highways. In the 1950s Greyhound Bus Lines featured a "5-Day Escorted Tour from Chicago Around Lake Michigan."

The official "Lake Michigan Circle Tour" route wasn't established until 1988 when the Great Lakes Commission approved a "Great Lakes Circle Tour" project. Attending the meeting were representatives from all eight Great Lakes tourism/travel groups, as well as governmental representatives. MDOT officials had already talked about a route around Lake Michigan in 1987 and within 14 months the route was planned and signs posted. The West Michigan Tourist Association published the first Lake Michigan Circle Tour booklet in 1988. Publicity about the new tour ran in the *Chicago Tribune* and the *Milwaukee Journal*, and 1,700 guidebooks were requested within three days of that media exposure.

The Lake Michigan Circle Tour is 1,092 miles long and circles the only one of the Great Lakes located entirely in the U.S. More than half of the tour is in Michigan, with about a third of the route in Wisconsin, while Illinois and Indiana each have about 5% of the circuit. Along the way there are more than 100 lighthouses, miles of beautiful beaches, charming harbor towns, Sleeping Bear Dunes National Lakeshore, and numerous state parks. The route crosses the mighty Mackinac Bridge, completed in 1957, and one of Michigan's most iconic structures. The route continues along the southern border of the Upper Peninsula hugging the top of Lake Michigan.

There are three branches of the Lake Michigan Circle Tour: the Harbor Tour in the Saugatuck/Douglas area; the Spur Route from Ludington to Manitowoc on the *S.S. Badger;* and the M-109 loop (D.H. Day Highway) in the Sleeping Bear Dunes area. While the rest of the Lake Michigan Circle Tour follows the closest trunkline to the big lake, the M-109 route is an exception. The brown "Lake Michigan Circle Tour Loop" sign designates the beginning of the M-109 loop at its southern junction with M-22 just northeast of Empire. The loop continues to Glen Haven, then returns to meet up with M-22 in Glen Arbor.

Leelanau Scenic Heritage Route

Michigan highways M-22, M-109 and M-204 in Leelanau County serve as both the major transportation arteries for Leelanau County residents as well as scenic routes for travelers and visitors. The scenic attractions and rural aspects of these roads motivated a group of concerned citizens to seek a Heritage Route designation from MDOT. In 2002, the group, after several years of working with the various townships and villages along the road, saw the Leelanau Scenic Heritage Route designated by the State legislature. The route includes all of M-22 in Leelanau County plus M-109 through Sleeping Bear Dunes National Lakeshore and M-204 which runs across the center of the county.

The group's mission statement reads: "The Heritage Route Committee is dedicated to promoting measures which protect and enhance the scenic, historical, and recreational characteristics of Michigan State Highways 22, 109, and 204 as they traverse the rural countryside and unique communities of Leelanau County." Committee members include representatives from Leelanau County, each township and village along the route, Sleeping Bear Dunes National Lakeshore, the Grand Traverse Band of Ottawa and Chippewa Indians, MDOT, various organizations and private citizens. MDOT explains that the Scenic Heritage Route designation ensures that "the rural character of the county remains in its current state and is managed in a manner that highlights the intrinsic qualities of the peninsula."

The 70-mile route offers some of the county's most spectacular vistas. The roads travel through rural areas of farms, orchards and vineyards. Small towns and villages along the route present charming shops and restaurants, tree-lined streets, attractive homes and cottages, roadside parks and picnic spots. There are brief glimpses of Lake Michigan through the trees, as well long stretches with views of its open water. Several small lakes and rivers can be seen along the route.

The Michigan Heritage Route System was established by Public Act 69 of 1993. Since then MDOT has approved sixteen heritage routes. In December 2014 the State legislature approved a change to rename the trunklines in the system as "Pure Michigan Byways." The change would allow the State to comply with federal regulations which require the "route" to be changed to "byway," and also provide a promotional tie-in to the popular Pure Michigan tourism campaign.

"Pure Michigan" Along Scenic M-22

"Pure Michigan" is found in breathtaking vistas along M-22 as it rambles along miles of untouched shoreline of Lake Michigan and Grand Traverse Bay. The road wanders through woodlands surrounding some of America's most beautiful lakes, rivers and streams. M-22 is the gateway to the towering sand dunes of Sleeping Bear and long stretches of sandy beach. Traversing the rural landscape the road passes picturesque farms, orchards and vineyards.

Chapter Two

Manistee County

"High tableland shore looking over the restless, horizonless expanse of the Big Sea Waters - that is Manistee County. Hills, orchards, wonderfully fair inland lakes - that is Manistee County. Rivers that are the haunts of gamey bass; rivers that broaden into hill-girt lakes buried in the woods - that is Manistee County. Brooks and creeks where lurk the wily trout, speckled and rainbow, waiting to do battle with venturesome fishermen - that is Manistee County. Views and scenic spectacles of far-flung broken country, of fascinating wilds, of waters and heights - that is Manistee County. Paved highways, smooth drives amidst rare beauties, sand trails winding into the maze of new forest - that is Manistee County."

-West Michigan Vacation Directory, 1929

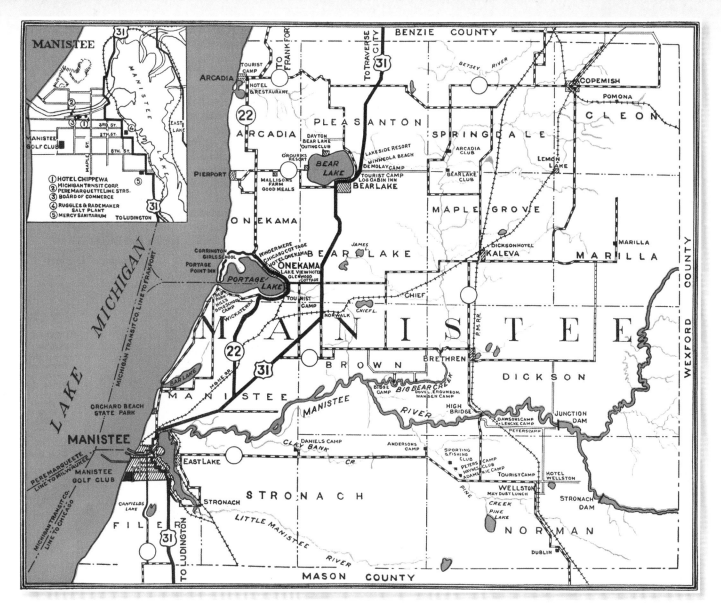

Scenic M-22 in Manistee County

"The scenic drive, M-22, leaves US-31 outside of Manistee, rounds the eastern end of Portage Lake, through Onekama on its shores, and among dunes to Arcadia. This is the old Chippewa Trail. From the high point, Arcadia in its valley, girt about with forested hills and high sand dunes, is a view hard to equal, although all of M-22 is beautiful."

-*West Michigan Vacation Directory*, 1930

A GLIMPSE OF PORTAGE LAKE HIGHWAY 22 ONEKAMA, MICH. 3385

Along Scenic M-22

"North from Manistee, along scenic M-22, is a vast vacation and resort development around Portage Lake, a land-locked harbor connected by a ship canal with Lake Michigan. Between the two lakes is Portage Point, site of a beautiful resort hotel, rental cottages and summer homes. On the north side of Portage Lake is Onekama, a renowned vacation center. Here are many flowing wells, a good shopping center and excellent resorts."

-Carefree Days in West Michigan, 1952

O-Nek-A-Ma
Meaning "Place of Great Beauty"

"When you are contemplating an enjoyable vacation, come to Onekama, on beautiful Portage Lake. A better location for a village and for resorting could not have been planned. It is swept by cool breezes off Lake Michigan, and surrounded by hills. Many springs and natural flowing wells provide the residents with healthy water."

-Manistee Vacation Guide, 1939

Onekama

The first village one encounters as one turns onto M-22 north of Manistee is Onekama on Portage Lake. The village had its beginning in 1845 as the settlement of Portage when the Stronach family built a sawmill on Portage Creek between Portage Lake and Lake Michigan. Landowners along the land-locked lake were not pleased when Stronach built a dam which periodically flooded their land. In 1871 a ditch was dug between the two lakes to prevent the Portage Lake water level from being artificially raised. This small opening gave way to a rush of water, lowering the lake level 12 to 14 feet, bringing it to the same level as Lake Michigan. The channel, increased to a width of 400 feet, was deep enough to accommodate boats and was maintained by the U.S. Government as a harbor of refuge.

ONEKAMA, MICH.   N-1840

With this change in the landscape, the settlement around the old Portage outlet was moved to the eastern end of Portage Lake. When the first post office was established in 1871, the community took the name of Onekama. The village of Onekama grew in a long narrow strip along the lakeshore with the business section on the flat, former lake bottom. Houses and other buildings were built on higher land. Onekama was incorporated as a village in 1891.

As lumbering died out in the state, new means of economic development were needed. In 1897 the Michigan State legislature enabled the formation of corporations that would develop resorts. In 1902 the Portage Point Assembly incorporated and built the Portage Point Inn. A summer colony developed, served by steamships bringing vacationers from Chicago, Milwaukee and other midwestern cities.

By the 1920s, the automobile had become the main means of transportation. Motorists traveling on M-22 drove through the heart of Onekama's business district. As more and more travelers discovered the appeal of this quaint village, more hotels, resorts and cottages were built to accommodate them. Gas stations, restaurants and stores catered to the needs of the motoring public. The charming village of Onekama still attracts travelers today as they head north on scenic M-22.

Onekama Merchants

"The Onekama retail business takes on an important part in the maintenance of the area as a resort center. Continued improvements in stock and services assure vacationers on Portage Lake of obtaining the best available merchandise. A courteous and friendly reception awaits you on 'Main Street' in Onekama."

-Manistee County, Michigan, 1952

LEE'S COFFEE SHOP
Scenic Route M-22—7-mi. from U. S. 31
Onekama, Mich.

Onekama Has Up-to-date Stores

*All Vacation Needs Anticipated
as well as Regular Stocks.*

Shoes, Clothing, Ready-to-wear
Groceries, Meats, Fresh Fruits, Vegetables
Hardware, Paints
Pottery, Souvenirs, Post Cards
Gas and Oils

GOOD HOTELS

You will find plenty of Summer Recreation
amid friendly surroundings.

*Swimming,
Motor Boating,
Tennis,
Dancing
Summer Theatre
Five Churches*

Portage Lake connects with Lake Michigan
by government constructed channel making
ideal harbor for yachts.

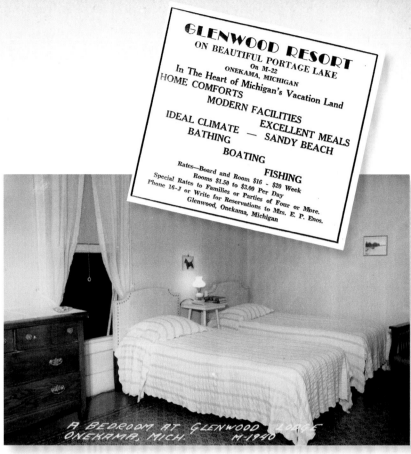

A BEDROOM AT GLENWOOD LODGE
ONEKAMA, MICH. M-1940

Glenwood Resort

"Glenwood Resort has three main buildings: Glenwood Lodge, Glenwood Annex and Glenwood Dining Hall. The Annex consists entirely of sleeping rooms newly furnished and beds have the best of innerspring mattresses. The Dining Room is clean, light, airy, and a pleasant view can be had from any window. You will enjoy your meals here. Wide verandas encircle the front and sides of buildings which face the blue waters of Portage Lake and Glenwood Beach....

All buildings at Glenwood are supplied from our own artesian flowing well - good, pure, cold water known for its healthful qualities.... Sufferers from heat and asthma find quick relief at Glenwood. The prevailing winds cross Lake Michigan and Portage Lake to Glenwood, giving us clean, pure, invigorating air, cool and delightful here when it is hot elsewhere....

You will get good food and plenty of it at Glenwood. Meals are prepared in homelike style, the best that the neighborhood farms afford in the way of fruits, vegetables, eggs, milk, chickens and other provisions.... Rates for room and board range from $32.50 to $37.50 per week. Special rates for families."

-Glenwood Resort, Onekama, Michigan on Portage Lake, circa 1930

GLENWOOD DINING HALL
ON PORTAGE LAKE - ONEKAMA MICH.   33835

SPRENGER HOTEL ONEKAMA, MICH. L-1836

Sprenger's Resort Lakeview Hotel

"Lakeview Hotel - the ideal resort hotel ... is considered more than a hotel by our guests; it is their summer home, where they renew acquaintances and make new friendships....

We are located at the edge of the Village of O-nek-a-ma ... but a few feet from Portage Lake, one of Michigan's finest.

Women do our cooking. They have helped make our place famous for its meals. We buy only the best meats. From Lake Michigan we get fresh trout and whitefish. From the surrounding farms and orchards we get fresh vegetables and fruits ... and we serve abundantly and graciously.

We accommodate 60 guests. We are not so large that we can't give personal attention and service to all our guests....

Onekama is a healthful spot. Close to Lake Michigan we have the benefit of the water-washed air ... being inland, that cold air is tempered by the sand dunes that lie along the coast. We have a countryside of flowing wells of pure water.... We are in cherry and fruit country. Our farms produce rich dairy and poultry products.... Many come here for hay fever relief."

-Sprenger's Resort Lakeview Hotel, circa 1930

SPRENGER'S RESORT

Lakeview HOTEL

O·NEK·A·MA, MICHIGAN

ON *Beautiful Portage Lake*

Onekama is an Indian name meaning "PLACE OF GREAT BEAUTY"

Little Eden Camp

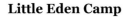

"Nestled between the hills and the shore of Portage Lake, one and one-half miles west of Onekama (follow the lake), you will find LITTLE EDEN CAMP, with its spacious grounds almost as mother nature made it.

The camp has good water on the grounds from flowing wells, modern rest rooms, fair swimming, with a beautiful winding road leading to a wonderful beach on Lake Michigan....

Stores are convenient, only one and one-half miles into Onekama. Milk is delivered daily and fresh vegetables delivered twice weekly on the grounds. Cottages are equipped for cooking. Home cooking served family-style, very reasonable, in the dining hall, if desired.

Large playgrounds for such sports as ball, croquet, horseshoes, running and jumping. Also free tennis courts and new playground equipment for children, as well as a large outdoor fireplace for weiner roasts, etc., and hot and cold shower baths.

Yes, it is a LITTLE EDEN just as the name implies - trees, flowers, brooks, birds, fishes, frogs, EVEN THE APPLE TREE (which is, NO ALCOHOLIC BEVERAGES or WILD PARTIES are permitted at any time), thus making an ideal place to bring your family for a vacation."

-Little Eden Camp, Onekama, Michigan, circa 1930

Exclusive Tent-Houses

"Camp Delight enjoys plenty of cool shade by day and cool, comfortable nights. The exclusive tent-houses are instantly adaptable to every weather condition.... Camp Delight's tent-houses are screened-in making them bug proof yet allowing any amount of ventilation. All are equipped with sanitary spring cots and every convenience for the camper."

-Camp Delight - In the Heart of Vacationland, circa 1924

Camp Delight

"Situated among the trees on the shore of beautiful Portage Lake, Camp Delight is one of the most unique and popular summer resorts in Western Michigan. Practically every outdoor sport may be enjoyed at Camp Delight.... Meals of good, wholesome, fresh food are known throughout the resort section, carefully prepared and served in a large, light, well-ventilated dining hall. Camp Delight has its own artesian well of pure, cold water.... The evening camp fires on the shore of the lake are a fitting close to many a perfect day at Camp Delight.... Besides being one of the finest spots to spend your vacation, Camp Delight is also one of the least expensive. Our rates are $15 and $18 per week. These rates include a comfortably furnished tent-house, all meals, use of camp equipment such as tennis courts, boats, etc."

-Camp Delight - In the Heart of Vacationland, circa 1924

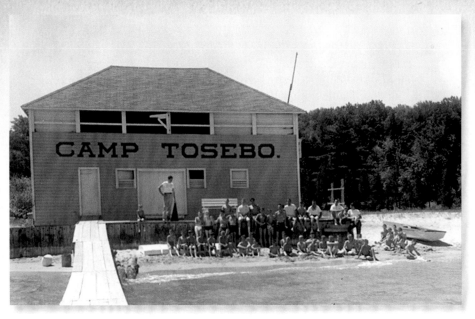

Camp Tosebo on Portage Lake Onekama, Mich. 246-K

Camp Tosebo for Boys

"This summer at Camp Tosebo you will travel by canoe as the Indians once did down the same shimmering streams and rivers through peaceful meadows and game-filled forests. You will pitch your tent, cook over an open fire, and then sleep under the star-studded heavens.

You will feel the thrill of silently gliding over rippling water beneath glistening white sails.... You will ride western style in the land of the deer and the squirrel through lovely stands of birch and pine....

You'll find plenty of chance for participation and instruction in baseball, tennis, archery, volleyball, basketball, track, pewee golf and football....

You may like to fish for perch, rock bass, or black bass. At the Water Carnival you will be able to display your skills at swimming, rowing, canoeing, sailing, and water skiing....

The woods and water and meadows at Tosebo offer ample opportunity for studying nature..."

-*Camp Tosebo*, circa 1965

Harmony Camp
Tourists Cottages and Cabins

On Waters Edge — Portage Lake

ONEKAMA, MICHIGAN

Beautiful Woodland Grove
Clean Sandy Beaches
Fine Bathing

... Sun and Shade as You Like It ...

— RATES —

$10.00 TO $ 00

PER WEEK

Harmony Camp

Located on the north side of Portage Lake, in a "beautiful woodland grove," Harmony Camp offered 14 modern cottages, all equipped for light housekeeping and accommodating from two to six persons. The cottage colony featured modern plumbing, gas, electricity, innerspring mattresses and electric refrigerators. It advertised that it had "State approved drinking water from artesian wells and mineral springs."

Portage Point Inn

The Portage Point Inn was built in 1902 by the Portage Point Assembly, a group of local investors. It was one of the first developments along the pristine shores of Portage Lake. The Inn was built with 30 guest rooms and constructed in six weeks by the same builder who built the Grand Hotel on Mackinac Island. A larger hotel was built in 1914, south of the original inn. Other buildings were added to the resort, including cottages and a dance pavilion, later known as the casino.

In 1914 management of the Inn was taken over by the Northern Michigan Transit Company. A dock brought the company's steamships practically to the front door of the Inn. The Portage Point Inn prospered for about 80 years. Legend has it that it was the place to go during Prohibition when alcohol was shipped in from Canada.

Guests had a wide range of activities from which to choose, including tennis, shuffleboard, bridge parties, dancing, bonfires on the beach, boating, sailing, sun bathing and swimming. Golf and horseback riding were available nearby.

Portage Point Inn has changed hands several times in the last two decades and still stands proudly facing Portage Lake. It is listed on the National Register of Historic Places.

A Class by Itself

"Far from the cares and worries of rushing city life, located on the shores of two of the most beautiful lakes, Portage Point Inn awaits you. Incomparable in setting; a high range of heavily wooded hills towering imposingly skyward in the rear of the Inn; before it - like a gem scintillating sapphire blue - is Portage Lake. Less than a block away the surf of mighty Lake Michigan majestically rolls up to a wide beach of crystal clear sand.

Come! Enjoy hours of carefree abandon or quiet, restful solitude. There's not a care in the world for you at Portage Point. Meals of Epicurean delight; a room, or a suite, of restful comfort; and a complete trained hotel staff to fulfill your every wish.

Spacious verandas, cool and shaded, overlooking Portage Lake. An ideal spot to spend an hour or two with a book or afternoon bridge. Cheery lobbies and recreation rooms assure the Inn's guests plenty of activity even on a rainy afternoon.

... A refuge for hay fever sufferers! A boon to the convalescent! A joy to the rugged and healthy! It is no wonder that children and grown-ups alike think of Portage Point as a summer paradise.... The Portage Point Inn is in a class by itself among the summer hotels of the Central West."

-Portage Point Inn, "Among Michigan's Finest," circa 1935

Postcard message:

Having a grand trip. The lakes are beautiful. Our cottage is in the woods. We got rather sunburned yesterday so taking it easy today. The weather here is comfortable, always a nice pleasant breeze.

-Bessie

Postmarked Onekama, 1946
Mailed to Austin, Texas

31

BIRDSEYE VIEW OF PIERPORT

Pierport

Pierport lies a few miles north of Onekama, just west off M-22 on the shores of Lake Michigan. The settlement was called Turnersport when its first post office opened in 1868, but the name was changed to Pierport in 1872. At one time Pierport was a bustling lumber town, but is now a resort community of summer homes and cottages.

Arcadia
Ideal Vacation Spot

"Arcadia, in the extreme north western part of Manistee County is ideally located for the vacationist who wishes to combine the pleasures of Lake Michigan with small lake accommodations and forest enjoyment.

The waters of Lake Michigan practically beat against the limits of the village. Here one may enjoy the miles of beach, far from the crowd of sightseers who attend the more populated places. Firewood is at hand for bonfires for beach parties, and one may hike for miles on the clean sands, or climb the dunes for sights that reward one handsomely for the effort.

If the big lake is too rough for enjoyment, and one wishes the quieter waters, then Arcadia Lake, also close at hand, will fulfill all desires. The water is clean and warm, the shores sloping and safe.

Arcadia is surrounded by woods, some of it virgin timber and the many quiet drives through its green hills and valleys offer to the tired city dweller rest and relaxation from the cares and troubles of a busy world. Wild life is here in abundance, be it birds or deer..."

-Manistee Vacation Guide, 1939

MAIN St. LOOKING EAST — ARCADIA MICH-13-

Up-To-Date Arcadia

"Just 22 miles north of Manistee is Arcadia, located on the shores of Lake Michigan, and a small inland lake. State Trunk Line M-22 ... runs through the town. Arcadia is a modern little town of about 800 inhabitants. It has electric light and power, up-to-date merchants, auto garages, drug store, bank, physician, and other facilities for serving its inhabitants and the tourist.... Arcadia gets the cool and invigorating breezes right off Lake Michigan. Its climate is healthful."

-Manistee, Michigan on the Scenic Paved Highway, M-11 - US-31, circa 1930

Business Life of Arcadia

Arcadia, at the time M-22 first passed through town, was a lively town with general stores, a hardware store, a drug store, a hotel, a bank, a newspaper, churches, and beautiful homes. The main businesses in town were related to the lumber industry with the Starke Land and Lumber Company and Arcadia Furniture Company being the main trades. The Starke company store was located at the foot of Lake Street. About 1930, Henry Behrens took over the store, after having been partners with Starke in the retail business.

Thompson's Service Station & Lunch Room

Ed Thompson took advantage of the increasing traffic on M-22 and opened a gas station with lunch room at the northeast corner of Lake Street and Sixth Street (M-22) selling Mobil gas. Note the visible register gas pumps that showed the customer just how much gas he was getting. The building later became a Texaco station.

Walther League Camp - Camp Arcadia

The Walther League Camp, also known as Camp Arcadia, was established in 1923 on the shores of Lake Michigan. Henry Starke, the local lumber baron and a dedicated Lutheran, purchased 30 acres of land for the purpose of establishing a Lutheran summer camp. The Walther League (the Lutheran Church Missouri Synod's national youth organization) added an additional 80 acres and started the camp as a "young person's training camp," but soon welcomed people of all ages. The camp continued to operate under the auspices of the Walther League until 1968, when the newly formed Lutheran Camp Association, purchased the camp and has operated it since 1969.

Postcard message:

Dear Grace & Louis,
We arrived at Arcadia Thursday July 1. Nice town, everybody fine. The roads are swell, no trouble. Could have arrived a day sooner. Enjoyed every mile. Looking forward to a nice, quiet, busy time here at the camp.
-John

Postmarked Arcadia, 1937
Mailed to Altadena, Calif.

SCENIC TURNOUT ON M-22 BETWEEN ARCADIA & FRANKFORT, MICH. 71085

Scenic Turnout

Highway M-22 winds through some of the state's most stunning scenery. This view, looking south from the scenic turnout north of Arcadia, presents a fine panorama of Lake Michigan and the surrounding hills and country. A short hike to the top of the nearby hill offers an even more spectacular view. Picnic tables and a path down to the lake make this a favorite stopping place for motorists.

Postcard message:

Wednesday, August 4th I think!
Hello,
We saw this lovely view from the top of a high hill. It is lovely! This is beautiful vacation country. We hike and swim every day and golf occasionally. How does this sound? 55 degrees at night, about 70 during the day. I'm staying two weeks & having a wonderful time.
-Marjorie

Postmarked Arcadia, date not legible
Mailed to Evanston, Ill.

SCENIC DRIVE ON M-22 ARCADIA, MICH.

Watervale on Herring Lake. Arcadia, Mich.

Watervale on Herring Lake, Arcadia, Mich.

Watervale Inn and Cottages

"Twenty-five years ago, on the south shore of Herring Lake, in Benzie County, there was a busy logging community, with a humming saw-mill, a railroad, a general store and comfortable dwellings. But the logging and lumbering operations have ceased, industry has passed on, leaving the village of Watervale in a delightfully quaint and semi-wild state....

Watervale has attractions to the devotee of water sports as well as for the one who takes his pleasure on shore. A concrete tennis court, pool and billiard tables, card rooms and a dance casino are provided. Herring Lake, a mile and a half long and a mile wide, has a beautiful sandy beach, ideal for bathing. It is connected to Lake Michigan by a channel wide enough for gasoline launches. It is also connected with upper Herring Lake by Herring Creek. Both lakes abound in fish....

Rates - $16 and $18 per week, $3 per day. Children under ten years of age, half rate.

Cottages - $150 and $200 for season, $75 per month; renters to furnish linen, silver and blankets."

-Watervale Inn and Cottages, Watervale, Mich.
circa 1925

Resort Colonies

"Entering Benzie County from the south and following the Lake Michigan coast line, is the famous M-22 scenic highway. This road passes through the resort colonies of the Herring Lakes, famed for their walleyed pike fishing, and continues north to Elberta."

-Carefree Days on West Michigan, 1945

Salsgiver's
Resort on Upper Herring Lake

Two miles east on good gravel road, leaving M-22 about three miles south of Elberta and Frankfort

Cottages	Camp Grounds	Boats

•

Good Fishing for

Wall-eyed Pike, Bass and Perch

•

Well Wooded Camp Grounds on Lake Shore

D. D. SALSGIVER, Prop.   Elberta, Mich., R. F. D.

Benson's Lakeland Cabins

Mr. and Mrs. W. Benson operated these cabins, located one mile south of Elberta. They advertised overnight and housekeeping cabins, modern facilities, and also tourist rooms. The cabin colony was only a quarter mile from Lake Michigan.

Elberta

The village of Elberta had its beginning as Frankfort City in 1866, but the name was changed to South Frankfort in 1872 when the first post office was established. Frankfort occupied the north side of Frankfort Harbor (Betsie Lake), while South Frankfort was on the south side. The village of South Frankfort was incorporated in 1874, then in 1911 the community changed its name to Elberta, named for the locally abundant Elberta peach.

The Frankfort Iron Furnace Company produced pig iron in the 1870s, but ceased operation when the expense of shipping in the ore from the Lake Superior region became too expensive. The property was passed to the Ann Arbor Railroad Company which in 1892 initiated car ferry operations from Lake Betsie to Kewaunee, Wisconsin. Later service ports included Manitowoc in Wisconsin and Menominee and Manistique in Michigan. The Ann Arbor Railroad yards and car ferry docks were located in the village limits of Elberta. The car ferries created a constant buzz of activity for 90 years, until 1982 when the operation was terminated.

Elberta was one of the largest centers for shipping fruit in the region. It also had a cannery for processing cherries. While an industrial town for most if its life, Elberta has transitioned to serve the growing numbers of vacationers in the area with stores and restaurants. Scenic M-22 passes through the heart of this pleasant village.

Elberta Life Saving Station

In 1887, soon after the Frankfort Harbor was dredged and piers were built, the U.S. Life Saving Service built a station on the Elberta side of the harbor, about 500 yards west of its current location. In 1934 the U.S. Coast Guard built a new station on the Frankfort side of the harbor. The old Elberta station was purchased in 1936 by the Ann Arbor Railroad and converted into its Marine Terminal Building.

The old wooden structure was originally designed to be moveable as sand and surf took their toll on the building. A lookout tower was accessed from the crew's living quarters by climbing a ladder. When an alarm rang, the surfmen would raise a trap door on the floor and slide down a pole fireman-style directly into the boat house. In 1990 the Elberta station was moved to its current site as part of the newly created Waterfront Park. The village of Elberta renovated the building for rental use for weddings and other events.

Elberta Mountain
Thrills for Spectators as Well as Skiers

"TWO OF THE LONGEST SKI JUMPS in the lower peninsula of Michigan are the center of interest at Elberta Mountain, a municipally-developed winter sports area in the Lake Michigan sand dunes within the village limits of the town on M-22, across Betsie Lake from Frankfort. In addition to the jumps, Elberta Mountain has numerous ski runs, served by an elaborate series of rope tows, which enable the ski jumpers to mount the steep hill to the takeoff level. Toboggan jumping has also become a popular sport on the Elberta hills.

A comfortable shelter house is situated in the center of the area and lunches and refreshments are served on weekends....

Outstanding ski jumpers from all sections of the middle west gather at Elberta Mountain several times during the winter for exhibition jumps. Ragnar Robertson, who learned ski jumping in his native Norway, serves as ski and jumping instructor."

-Winter Sports in West Michigan, circa 1956

Elberta Beach

"Elberta is separated from Lake Michigan by gigantic sand dunes which are the delight of explorers of all ages. Bathing can be enjoyed in Lake Michigan. Some of the largest and finest perch are caught along the docks and from the breakwater extending out into Lake Michigan."

-Benzie County Fishing and Vacation Guide, 1941

Elberta, Mich.

Elberta Beach & Harbor
Elberta, Mich.

Postcard message:

Dear Grace:-
Was along here today - Not a one in sight - only gulls. Ah! What hills up here. The scenery is beautiful. Lake and beach just lovely. We are all just dandy and enjoying every minute of this trip.

Love, Floyd & Maude

Postmarked Elberta, 1949
Mailed to Jackson, Mich.

Frankfort on Scenic M-22

"Scenic highway M-22 passes through the center of Frankfort on its winding way along the Lake Michigan shore. Here can be found scenes to warm the heart of any photographer be he amateur or professional."

-Benzie County Vacationland, 1953

Frankfort Gateway

The gateway to Frankfort has been a landmark since it was built in 1925. The original structure was in downtown Frankfort at the corner of Main and Seventh Streets. Its columns were built of stones from Lake Michigan to resemble lighthouses and the connecting arch supported a model of the new, modvern Ann Arbor No. 7 car ferry, which had sailed into the Frankfort harbor earlier that year. In 1937 when street and sewer work required the landmark to either be razed or moved, the City Council voted to dismantle and rebuilt it at the top of the hill on M-115 overlooking the city and harbor. The basic design remained the same, but concrete was used for the pillars instead of stone. In 1964 the car ferry replica was remodeled to resemble the newer *City of Green Bay* car ferry. Over the years the arch has had different wording, including the original "Frankfort," also "Frankfort -the Resort Town of Michigan," and "Frankfort - A Growing Resort City." Twice the panel referred to roads including our favorite, "Scenic M-22 Road," and the later "Scenic M-115.

U.S. Coast Guard, Frankfort, Mich.

Frankfort's Harbor

The U.S. Government initiated dredging a channel from Betsie Lake to Lake Michigan as early as 1859. By 1873 the channel was 200 feet wide with two 600-foot piers. A depth of about nine feet allowed most marine traffic to enter the harbor. In 1873 a light was constructed on the north pier to mark the harbor entrance. In 1887 a life saving station was built on the Elberta side. The piers were extended in 1912 until they were about 2,000 feet in length and a new steel lighthouse was erected on the north side. Breakwaters were built about 1930 to shelter the harbor and the old piers were shortened. In 1932 the lighthouse was moved from the north pier to the head of the north breakwater. It was increased in size by placing it on top of a new 25-foot square steel base and upgraded to a Fourth Order Fresnel lens. In 1934 a new U.S. Coast Guard station was built on the Frankfort side of the channel, standing guard for all marine traffic.

Postcard message:

We reached here at 7 o'clock Wed nite. Have a nice place to stay. We are taking the boat in the morning at 6 o'clock for Manistique - a 7 hour trip.

-Olga & Myron

Postmarked Frankfort, 1947
Mailed to: Grass Lake, Mich.

U.S. Coast Guard Station, Frankfort, Mich.

Frankfort - The Finest Beach on Lake Michigan

"This is one of Michigan's great port towns ... located on the shores of Lake Michigan and Betsie Bay at the foot of the great Sleeping Bear dune region. We are on Scenic Highway M-22 in a region whose economy is wrapped up in fruit farms and in hospitality to those seeking recreation. Our beach of singing sands is the cleanest and finest along the entire coast of Michigan. Our summer sun is tempered by the water-washed air that comes over cool Lake Michigan - a truly delightful climate. We offer you accommodations in good resort hotels, cabins, cottages and rooming houses. Our modern business houses offer you every service."

-Carefree Days in West Michigan, 1949

Marine Ballroom

The Marine Ballroom was located one and a half miles from Frankfort on M-22. It was a popular dance pavilion with a modern amplifying system and the largest dance floor in the area. Advertised as the "most palatial dance pavilion in Northern Michigan," it featured dancing every night in the summer. The dance hall and beer garden was owned and operated by Elliott Jacobsen from the late 1920s to the mid-1930s. One of the popular bands featured was Ken Stone and His Revellers, who played at the Mayfair Hotel in Miami during the winter months.

Famous Mineral Springs

"... the fast becoming famous mineral well [is] situated in the heart of Municipal Park, in the village of Frankfort.... September 24, 1885, it underwent the first rigid analysis. It was found to contain the following ingredients, so carefully proportioned and compounded by nature's own Pharmacist as to make it one of the most valuable of mineral waters: Sulphate of Lime, Sulphate of Magnesia, Sulphate of Soda, Chloride of Potassium, Chloride of Magnesia, Oxide of Iron, Soluble Salicia. Step by step this wonderful water, with no other advertising but its own merits, has worked its way into a nation-wide publicity. Hundreds of people from every state in the Union visit this well and derive the benefits of its wonderful health giving properties."

-*Northern Michigan Magazine*, February 1928

Metropolis of Benzie County

Frankfort was first settled in 1850 by Joseph Oliver. It is said that one of the early residents remarked that the area reminded him of Frankfort, Germany, and suggested the name for the village. A post office was established in 1860 and the village was incorporated in 1885. For several years the county seat was in Frankfort. The village population saw a steady growth and in 1935 Frankfort became a city. It still is the largest population center in Benzie County.

Like many northern Michigan towns, Frankfort's early commerce depended on lumbering, followed by fishing and tourism. The early hotels and boarding houses mainly served lumbermen and mariners. The monumental Royal Frontenac, built in 1902, attracted vacationers coming by rail to the Elberta-Frankfort area. Although the hotel burned in 1912, it helped to establish the region as a vacation destination. Other hotels were built in Frankfort, and resorts and cottages were constructed on the nearby lakes.

Amenities attracting vacationers were golf courses, boating and sailing facilities, bathing beaches, fine fishing, and scenic drives. A movie theater, dance halls, tennis courts, shuffleboard and miniature golf offered amusements. Frankfort became known as the metropolis of Benzie County with its selection of fine stores, cultural advantages and recreational opportunities.

Park Hotel

"Here is a unique Michigan summer resort where you can always enjoy a cool breeze from Lake Michigan. Hay Fever sufferers find this the ideal spot for relief as it is the most invigorating climate along the lake.... The pine-scented air is a bracing tonic that refreshes you for another day and builds up a store of energy and smooths out frayed nerves.... Frankfort's swimming, bathing and beach facilities are without equal. One of the finest beaches to be found on Lake Michigan is located just north of the breakwater.... The finest foods are served quietly and courteously in our dining room. You will like the air of dignity, the excellent foods and the moderate prices. Spacious restful lobbies with every modern convenience and comfort."

-Park Hotel - Frankfort, Michigan, circa 1940

The New East Shore Hotel

"The only hotel built in the U.S.A. during the year 1933. Located only two blocks from the finest bathing beach on the east coast of Lake Michigan.

'The 7 Spot' - Our Cocktail Lounge and Sandwich Shop - next door to the theatre.

A.E. (Park) Herren, Mgr. - Dale R. Herren, Asst. Mgr.

In Frankfort, the Resort Town of Michigan. Open All Year - Phone 4731"

-postcard back, circa 1935

Garden Theatre

The Garden Theatre in Frankfort opened in 1923 during the age of silent films. It has been in almost continuous use ever since. When it was built, the theatre was a showplace with 592 seats. It was modernized later with "700 deluxe seats ... RCA high fidelity sound and high intensity projection." This advertisement from 1948 proclaims "All new from street to screen." The theatre was purchased in 2008 by a community group, carefully renovated and reopened in 2009 to great fanfare.

Garden Theatre
FRANKFORT
All new from street to screen
700 DELUXE SEATS!
Our Seating Arrangement Makes
Perfect Vision from Each Seat
RCA High Fidelity Sound!
High Intensity Projection!
Shows Daily at 7:00 and 9:15 p.m.
Sunday Matinee at 3:00

Phone 4431

7 - Spot Cocktail Bar & Sandwich Shoppe

The 7-Spot was a popular stomping ground in downtown Frankfort for many years. It specialized in draught beer, fine wines, and mixed drinks. Menu items included steaks, fish, pork chops and sandwiches. Since it was next door to the Garden Theatre, it was a favored stop for moviegoers. In the 1930s and early 1940s dancing was featured every night except Sunday.

THE 7 SPOT
Frankfort's Finest
STEAKS — CHOPS — FISH
BEER — WINE — LIQUORS
John and Charles Weslock

55

National Glider Meet, Frankfort, Mich.

The Soaring Center of America

"…The Soaring Society of America decided to hold the first American Open Soaring Meet at Frankfort. The meet, held the last of August in 1938, was successful from every standpoint.

A group of local business men formed the Frankfort Soaring Association. This group induced Stan Corcoran … to go east and purchase a glider, later christened the 'City of Frankfort' and return with it to start instruction.

Another movement was on foot which resulted in the formation of the Frankfort School of Soaring, which had its first students in the summer school of 1939 among whom were twelve Government students whose training was paid for by the Government. The latter has come to realize that gliding is one of the essential steps toward training pilots for power ships.

Gliding is fast becoming a national sport and with the momentum it has now gained it looks as though soaring will eventually be the most outstanding sport in this section of Michigan. Frankfort is ideally located for soaring and gliding, and this will be an added attraction for the summer visitors, for with the school in operation, gliders will be in the air constantly."

-Benzie County Fishing and Vacation Guide, 1940

National Glider Meet. Frankfort. Mick.

Gliding

"You can learn to glide in a motorless glider, you can go as a passenger in a two-place glider, or you can just watch others glide at Frankfort on Lake Michigan. Motorless gliding is regarded as about the safest form of flying. There's no noise - just a quiet riding of air currents, often sliding sideways, now going up on a thermal, and again gliding slowly to earth. Frankfort claims to have the only commercial school to teach gliding in the country."

-McCracken's 1940 Guide to Michigan

M-22 at Crystal Lake

"Take the road, M-22, that runs along the north end of Crystal Lake. Here on a high ridge one glimpses to the south Crystal Lake and to the north one hears and sees Lake Michigan beating against the sandy shore many feet below. There are wooded heights, rolling valleys, golf courses and charming cottages."

-West Michigan Vacation Directory, 1930

Crystal Lake

"Crystal Lake is now recognized as not only the most beautiful lake of the many small lakes in which Michigan abounds, but also as unsurpassed if indeed unequaled, in the whole country.... Crystal Lake impresses all by its beauty and general attractiveness....

It is about nine miles in length from east to west, and two to two and a half miles average in width. It covers twenty square miles or more. It is surrounded by bluffs, lower and higher, mostly wooded. Its waters are remarkably clear and pure, its beaches wide and sandy, its waters shallow for a considerable distance out, rendering it especially favorable for bathing."

-The Crystal Lake and Platte Lakes Region,
circa 1925

Greetings from Beulah, Mich.
CRYSTAL LAKE
Gateway to Sleeping Bear National Park

BATHING BEACH CRYSTAL LAKE FRANKFORT, MICH. H.S.M.

BATHING BEACH CRYSTAL LAKE FRANKFORT, MICH. A-742

Postcard message:

July 6-
Sorry to hear that the heat and humidity continue in Chicago. We had the fireplace going this morning. Afternoons just right for swimming.

Vera, & Davey

Postmarked Frankfort, 1941
Mailed to Chicago, Ill.

CRYSTAL BEACH RESORT, FRANKFORT, MICH.

Crystal Beach Resort
(formerly Crystal Pautz Resort)

Located one mile east of the Congregational Summer Assembly on the south shore, this was the first resort on Crystal Lake. Crystal Beach Resort began its life as Crystal Banks, started by A.E. Banks. He built several cottages and a dock, then sold the property in 1891 to Robert Pautz, who had the money to purchase it after winning the Irish Sweepstakes. In its second life, the resort was known as the Crystal Pautz Resort and by the 1920s had nine cottages and a lodge. Mr. and Mrs. Pautz were happy to share their facilities with local people who were welcome to come for a day's picnic and swimming.

E.R. House was the next owner of the resort and changed the name to Crystal Beach Resort. By 1941 the cottage colony had grown to eleven cottages, all with electric lights, running water and inside toilets. The cottages were completely furnished except for linens and silverware. Some of the cottages had fireplaces, sunrooms, and multiple bedrooms. All had cooking stoves, some oil and some wood. There were also camp sites available with space for auto trailers. Hundreds of feet of private bathing beach were available for guests, as well as a bath-house, shuffleboard court, ping pong and other games. Boats were available to rent for fishing or excursions around the lake.

COTTAGES CRYSTAL BEACH RESORT CRYSTAL LAKE
FRANKFORT, MICH.

Crystalaire Camp for Girls
(formerly Osoha-of-the-Dunes)

"What We Believe: Living and Learning in the Out-of-Doors - appreciating the beauty of birch trees, dunes, cloud-filled skies, crystal waters, sunsets over Lake Michigan; ... taking trips combined with pioneer camping - cooking with a reflector oven, sleeping under the stars, running down steep sand dunes, living in a wilderness out-post, canoeing down rivers, horseback riding through woods and fields, and camping in the rain; learning to use an axe, knife and compass correctly; adventures and fun in the woods, fields and beaches of northern Michigan.... We believe that this can best be done by creating a happy environment where everyone is busily and actively doing the things she most enjoys."

-Crystalaire Camp for Girls, circa 1950

Active Waterfront

"Our active waterfront offers swimming instruction at all levels from beginner through Lifesaving, and campers may choose additional instruction in specialized swimming and diving. Our five canoes are used for instructional purposes and for the weekly canoe trips of advanced canoeists on the many Michigan rivers. Water skiing and sailing instructions are given."

-Crystalaire Camp for Girls,
circa 1950

M 22 along North Shore of
Crystal Lake "Pilgrim" Mich.   C-2595

—Bathing Beach—
Pilgrim   Mich.

Cong'l Summer Assembly, Pilgrim, Mich. Frankfort

The Congregational Summer Assembly

"The Congregational Summer Assembly was established in 1904. It has a property of about 120 acres at the southwest corner of Crystal Lake, extending a mile westward to Lake Michigan. It has a 'Lodge' for guests, a dining hall, auditorium, and a pavilion or summer store, and about 100 cottages. A number of these cottages are available for rent. The facilities for bathing, boating, and fishing are unsurpassed about the lake. The program of the Assembly, though not elaborate, usually includes some of the best specialists on subjects treated, Bible study being central. Prominence is given to music. An auto bus line makes several round trips from Frankfort, two miles to the south, to the Assembly every day during the season. While the Assembly is nominally under Congregational auspices, it is practically undenominational. All who seek rest and recreation, rather than a field in which to display the latest fashion, are cordially welcomed. Many of its regular summer residents and supporters are from other religious bodies."

-*The Crystal Lake and Platte Lakes Region*, circa 1925

Congregational Summer Assembly Lodge

"Rooms are available at the Lodge at rates varying from $9 per week for small rooms for one person to $25 per week for four people. While no rooms with bath are available, there are two bath rooms, one on each floor, and an ample supply of hot water is provided. The beds are comfortable, the lounge with its fireplace is very popular, and the spirit of friendliness makes a vacation at the Lodge a real success. Electric lights throughout reduce fire hazard, and flush toilets insure sanitation."

-Congregational Summer Assembly,
In 1947 Vacation with Us

Kindred Souls

"At the western end of Crystal Lake, on a wooded peninsula between its clear waters and the blue of Lake Michigan, is the Congregational Assembly. Here kindred souls gather to enjoy the multitude of summer pleasures afforded by the region and at the same time enjoy intellectual recreation and development."

-*West Michigan Vacation Directory*, 1924

Crystalia, Frankfort, Mich.

Crystalia

"Crystalia, just north of the Assembly, was started by Chicago parties.... Numerous cottages have been built along the lake front and also somewhat back in the woods. Along the west shore of the lake northward are many substantial cottages."

-*The Crystal Lake and Platte Lakes Region*, circa 1925

Postcard message:

Dear Neighbor,
This resort is not far from us, across Crystal Lake and looks very much as it does at our beach. We look from our side windows out upon the lake just a few steps from the cottage. The air is beautiful & so clear. Next week the lectures etc. will begin also concerts, marshmallow roasts, picnics & all sorts of entertainment for old & young. We have six roomers, all very pleasant people. Wish all our friends and neighbors could be here too.

Yours, Florence

Postmarked Frankfort, date not legible
Mailed to Elyria, Ohio

CRYSTALIA, MICH.

Three Pines Inn

The Three Pines Inn, guaranteed a "delightful outing on the shores of Crystal Lake and Lake Michigan." Located three miles from Frankfort, it offered rooms for rent and as well as housekeeping cottages. Known for its fine dining room service, the inn offered "pure milk," fresh fruits, vegetables and fish. Its Sunday chicken dinners were a popular weekly event.

Postcard message:

8/25/41
Dear Dad,
At Lansing Saturday night - here Sunday late afternoon. Made good time & had fine roads all the way. It's very nice here & plenty to keep you busy all the time. Hope everything is going OK.
Love, Lou

Postmarked Frankfort, 1941
Mailed to Cincinnati, Ohio

Point Betsie Lighthouse

The Point Betsie Lighthouse is located just off M-22, about four miles north of Frankfort. Situated on a prominent point, it was an important marker for mariners since it designated the spot where ships turned into, or away from, the Manitou Passage.

It was originally named *Pointe aux Becs Scies*, which means "sawed beak point" for the Sawbill or Merganser duck which was prevalent in the area. The lighthouse with a tower of 37 feet and a Fourth Order Fresnel lens was built in 1858. It was the last manned lighthouse on the eastern shore of Lake Michigan since it wasn't automated until 1983. In 2004 the Friends of Point Betsie Lighthouse rehabilitated the lighthouse and now operate it as a museum. Point Betsie is one of the most photographed lighthouses in the country because of its easy access, stunning beauty and dramatic setting.

Dunes at Point Betsie

"Blocking the way of Highway M-22 to the north from Frankfort and Crystal Lake is the great wall of earth known to geologists as the Point Betsie moraine.... The wooded dunes ... toward Point Betsie are blowouts, troughs, 'horseshoes,' moving sands, wooded islands, and drifting wastes. The dunes range in size from small ridges near the Point Betsie lighthouse, to hills of 200 feet or more."

-Stace, *Michigan's Mystic Dunes*, 1939

Saving Lives at Point Betsie

The high volume of marine traffic passing Point Betsie prompted the government to establish a U.S. Life Saving Station there. Designed by architect Francis W. Chandler, it was completed in 1876. The station was built to the south of the lighthouse, across the road. One of the most heroic and challenging rescues on Lake Michigan was conducted by the surfmen of the Point Betsie station in 1880 when the schooner *J.H. Hartzell* ran aground in a bitter storm about a mile south of the Frankfort harbor. With the exception of the ship's cook, who was weak with illness, the rest of the crew were courageously saved.

Point Betsey Life Saving Station, near Frankfort, Mich.
Copyright 1911 by Frank P. Wright.

U.S. LIFE SAVING STATION

U.S. Coast Guard.
Point Betsie.
Frankfort, Mich.

In 1915 the U.S. Life Saving Service transformed into the U.S. Coast Guard. Plans for a new building soon followed that transition and a new station, designed by architect Victor Mendleheff, was completed in October 1917. The old and new buildings, each with its own distinctive cupola-like tower, stood next to each other for about a month, then in November the old life saving building was demolished. After the Point Betsie Coast Guard Station was decommissioned in 1937, it was placed in the custody of the Frankfort Coast Guard Station, but is now privately owned.

Crystal Downs Golf Club, Frankfort, Mich.

Crystal Downs

"Crystal Downs, five miles north of Frankfort, [is] touched but not entered by state highway M-22. It is one of the rare places where the finest efforts of Nature and man may be found together.... With a Lake Michigan coastline of more than two miles, its five hundred acres of rugged forest, dune, and meadowland are located high on the narrow ridge of land separating Crystal Lake from the big lake. From anywhere on the property a magnificent view may be had of one lake or the other, or frequently both.... Surely the delight of variety is one of the first delights of Crystal Downs.

The Clubhouse, which is now under construction, will make use of an unsurpassed location in a very creditable manner. The building, a fine example of Old English, was designed by Alexander McColl of Grand Rapids, and much care is being given to the execution of the rough timber and masonry work to achieve the most attractive effect for this type of building."

-*Michigan Magazine*, May 1929

Postcard message:

All homes built in Crystal Downs must amount to $40,000 or more. Smaller amounts are not allowed. What could I do with 1/40 of that amount?

Postcard not mailed.

Crystal Downs Country Club, Frankfort, Mich.

D-556

Lake Michigan Summer Home Colony

"Crystal Downs is a most unusual summer residence ... and country club development, adjoining Michigan's premiere scenic highway, M-22.... It is unusual in its wealth of natural beauty and panoramic grandeur.... There are few places where so much thought is being given to the artistic and architectural harmony of each and every building...few places where nature and man have so successfully conspired to provide an extraordinary degree of the out-of-door enjoyment and recreation for which West Michigan is so justly famed.... There are only one hundred and seventy-six locations, each so choice as readily to warrant the building of a home of the high artistic standards to which all lots are restricted. You will be delighted with Crystal Downs."

-advertisement, *Michigan Magazine*, May 1929

Q-562 COTTAGE AT CRYSTAL DOWNS FRANKFORT, MICH.

CRYSTAL DOWNS GOLF CLUB FRANKFORT MICH.

Finest Golf Course

The Crystal Downs Country Club opened in 1928. A nine-hole golf course opened the following year. Dr. Alister MacKenzie and Perry Maxwell were hired to design a full eighteen-hole course which opened in 1933. The eighteen holes are laid out on a hilly narrows between Crystal Lake and Lake Michigan, with a steep bluff dropping down hundreds of feet to the big lake. MacKenzie was resistant to take on a project in northern Michigan, but after visiting the site, he acquiesced and designed one of the most challenging and natural looking courses in the country. Crystal Downs has consistently been rated in the top 100 courses in the nation.

Chimney Corners

"Chimney Corners, on the bluffs of the north shore of beautiful Crystal Lake, is a homelike resort in the popular summering region of northwest Michigan. The table which features home cooking, is largely supplied with vegetables, fruits and dairy products from our own garden and connecting farm. The dining room seats thirty guests and has a large fireplace and six windows overlooking the lake. The sleeping rooms are well cared for and airy. Good beds and blankets. Two rooms with fireplaces and private bath, also outside entrances are obtainable. Electricity throughout the house, grounds and cottages. A croquet court is on the grounds and tennis enthusiasts play for free on the public cement courts in Frankfort.... Chimney Corners is fortunate in being located just one mile from the famous scenic Crystal Downs Golf Course. The Congregational Assembly is but four miles, with its program of lectures and entertainments. The noted Interlochen Bowl with its delightful concerts is less than an hours drive. Point Betsie Light House and Lake Michigan Beach are but two miles distant and afford ideal spots for picnic dinners. The Platte River trip with motor boat service may be enjoyed at moderate cost."

-Chimney Corners - Crystal Lake North Shore, circa 1940

CHIMNEY CORNERS

Crystal Lake

North Shore

Mr. and Mrs. O. A. Rogers

Frankfort — Michigan

and

Edgewater — Florida

Ken-Tuck-U-Inn

Ken-Tuck-U-Inn was located on M-22 on Long Lake, just north of Crystal Lake. It was built by Bertie Bancroft, the son of Robert Bancroft, who was the founder of the lumbering town of Aral. When the lumbering business died out, Bertie Bancroft left Aral, but moved back to the area in 1925 .He purchased forty acres near Long Lake and built a large home, which also served as an inn and restaurant. The Inn offered lodging and camping and was known for its chicken dinners. The building still stands and is now part of the Sleeping Bear Dunes National Lakeshore.

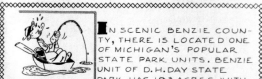

IN SCENIC BENZIE COUNTY, THERE IS LOCATED ONE OF MICHIGAN'S POPULAR STATE PARK UNITS. BENZIE UNIT OF D.H. DAY STATE PARK HAS 183 ACRES WITH FACILITIES FOR THOSE WHO ENJOY BOTH MODERN AND PRIMITIVE SURROUNDINGS.

IT IS SITUATED ON HIGHWAY M-22 12 MILES NORTHEAST OF FRANKFORT, 7 MILES NORTH OF BEULAH, 7 MILES NORTHWEST OF U.S. 31 AT HONOR AND 32 MILES SOUTHWEST OF TRAVERSE CITY.

ENJOY PICNICKING, CAMPING, SWIMMING, NATURE STUDY AND VARIOUS OTHER FUN-FILLED ACTIVITIES. THE PLATTE RIVER WHICH RUNS BY THE PARK, IS NAVIGABLE AND A FAVORITE SPOT FOR FISHERMEN. FOR BOATING ENTHUSIASTS THERE IS THE POPULAR "PLATTE RIVER FLOAT TRIPS AND GUIDED FISHING TRIPS", AS WELL AS BOAT LIVERIES WHERE THE CAMPER CAN RENT A BOAT.

FOR INFORMATION WRITE TO, MANAGER, D.H. DAY STATE PARK, GLEN ARBOR, MICHIGAN.

Recommended for Preservation

The site of Benzie State Park was one of the first sites recommended for preservation as a state park by the Michigan Natural Areas Advisory Council in the early 1920s. The park was established in 1923 with 180 acres, but improvements and access to the park were not completed until 1927. Over the next several decades more acres were added to the park. When Benzie State Park was absorbed into the Sleeping Bear Dunes National Lakeshore in 1975, it encompassed 2,255 acres of woods and dunes, a quarter mile of sandy beach on Lake Michigan, and substantial frontage on the Platte River.

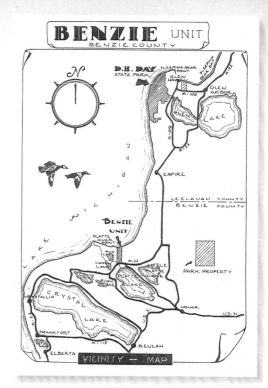

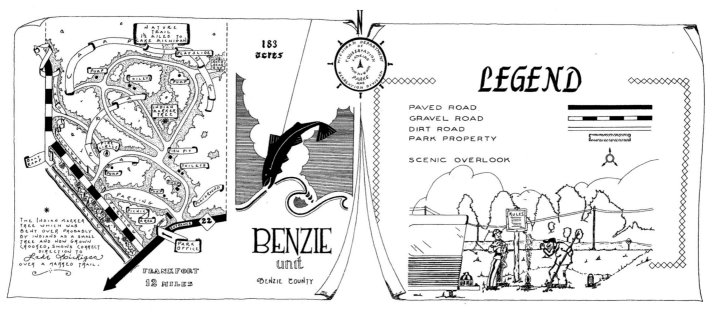

Benzie State Park

"Benzie State Park, located on M-22 at the Platte River, is owned and maintained by the Michigan Department of Conservation and is open free to the use of the public throughout the summer months with a capable, courteous attendant in charge.

The park as a whole takes in many acres with a wide frontage on Lake Michigan. It is heavily wooded, mostly with pine and oak, and includes along the big lake some of the most picturesque and truly wonderful sand dune formations in the country. The beach itself is a wide, gently sloping expanse of sand. From the park entrance directly back to Lake Michigan is but a short walk, hardly more than a mile....

The camp ground of the state park is located near the entrance where fine well water, rest rooms, playground equipment and picnic tables are supplied. A store is also operated by the park keeper supplying groceries and refreshments.

Boats are available nearby for fishing on Round Lake adjoining the park, and on the Platte Lakes, less than five minutes drive distant."

-Benzie County Fishing & Vacation Guide, 1938

The Store, Benzie State Park, M-22, Honor, Mich.

Amidon Tourist Station

"Happy" Amidon's Tourist Station was the original boat rental spot on the Platte River. Its waterwheel on the riverbank became a well-known landmark. The station also sold groceries, gas, and fishing supplies. Rowboats or canoes were used to cruise the delightful Platte downstream to the Lake Michigan beach.
The river trip was ideal for viewing the scenery and abundant wildlife near its shores. In the 1970s the station became the Waterwheel and offered tours on the the river on the *Paddle Princess*. In the 1960s Riverside Canoe Trips, located on the south side of the river, opened a canoe livery and camping supply store, which still provides a pleasant stop on M-22 for a relaxing trip on the river.

Platte River Boat Trip

"Float down this beautiful trout stream with the current to Lake Michigan, fish along the way if you like and be towed back by power boat. Many visitors make several trips, each one bringing out newly discovered beauty."

-*M-22 'The Manitou Trail'*, circa 1955

Platte River Playground

A favorite swimming and picnic area in the Benzie State Park was the beach where the Platte River winds its way into Lake Michigan. Camping, canoeing, fishing, hiking and wiener roasts were just as popular at the time this photo was taken (circa 1950) as they are today.

Chapter Four

Overlooking Glen Lake from the Sand Dunes 17

SLEEPING BEAR SAND DUNES FROM WEST END OF GLEN LAKE, MICH.—38

Leelanau County

"It is a region of wild scenic beauty, blue lakes, Indian and fishing villages, fruit orchards, beautiful homes, traveling sand dunes and friendly people. Native to it are Indians of the Ottawa and Chippewa tribes. Its summer climate is soft and pleasant because of its peninsular character. Its air is scented with the aroma of flowers and greenery. Its woods are full of deer and other wildlife. That's Michigan's Leelanau Peninsula.

Leelanau is an Indian word, meaning 'Land of Delight.' It is to the State of Michigan as the little finger is to the left hand, palm turning outward. It is reached via M-22 from Frankfort and the Crystal Lake Country, or by M-22 from Traverse City along Grand Traverse Bay. The highway around the peninsula, or 'around the horn,' as it is locally described, is one of the scenic drives in Michigan."

-*Motor News*, June 1955

M-22 through Leelanau County

"Leelanau has more than 100 miles
of scenic coastline highway . . . M-22 enters
Leelanau County south of Empire. From here
the road hugs the shoreline, rising into the hills
in many places, where magnificent views of the
lake shore and inland orchard and farm country
may be seen.

Local folks in the county may well boast
that they have the finest county road system
in Michigan. Few of the highways are straight,
because the county is one of gentle hills and
broad valleys . . . and the roads have been built
to follow the contour of the county in most
sections. Those who follow the highways . . .
and the byways . . . have water in sight most of
the time - either Lake Michigan along the west
side, Grand Traverse Bay on the east, or one of
the beautiful inland lakes or streams."

-Carefree Days in West Michigan, 1946

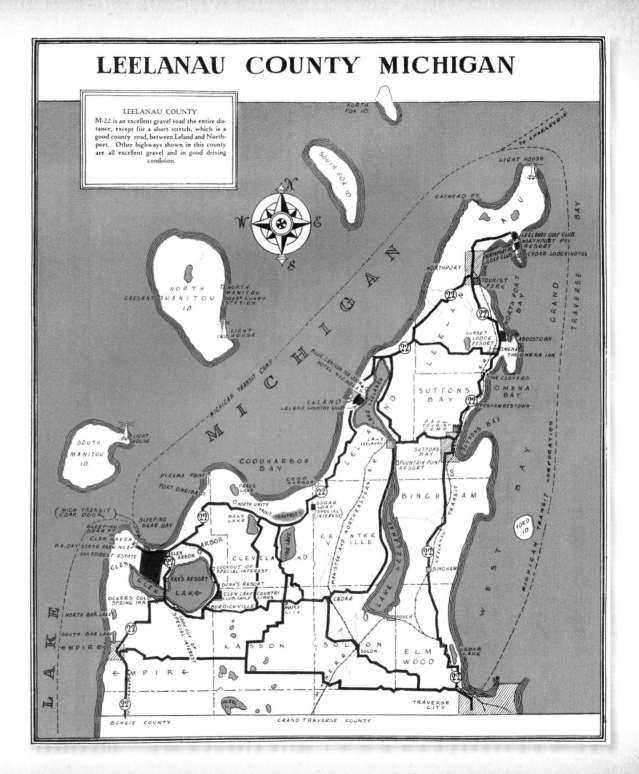

LEELANAU COUNTY MICHIGAN

LEELANAU COUNTY
M-22 is an excellent gravel road the entire distance, except for a short stretch, which is a good county road, between Leland and Northport. Other highways shown in this county are all excellent gravel and in good driving condition.

MIC·126

EMPIRE·Mich.

Empire from Orchard Hill.

The Bluff, Empire, Mich.

Empire's Majestic Views

"Highway M-22 climbs over the Empire moraine and descends a long, winding hill into a short, narrow valley. Here was an ancient bay, say the geologists, and the Empire dunes were built up on bars across its mouth.

From the shore hills of Empire, wonderful views delight the sight-seer. Across the broad bay to the south is Point Betsie, eleven miles away by water. Seven miles to the north is Sleeping Bear. Beyond Sleeping Bear, fifteen miles from Empire, is South Manitou Island, the silver cliffs of which gleam brightly in the sun."

-Stace, *Michigan's Mystic Dunes*, 1939

C-2666
M 22 AT EMPIRE MICH

Empire

It is generally believed that the village of Empire takes its name from two shipwrecks near the site of the present village. The side-wheeler *Empire State* went aground in 1849, and the schooner *Empire* was shipwrecked in 1865. The village was originally settled in 1852 by John LaRue, who purchased 40 acres from the U.S. Government. From this small beginning a modest little village grew, becoming an organized village in 1895.

As one heads into Empire from the north on M-22, the old schoolhouse is still standing on the left. The school was built in 1900 with four classrooms. Later more classrooms and a gymnasium were incorporated into the building. The school was used until 1967. Empire is a village filled with history: from the historical buildings lining its main street to the museum complex to the historical marker at the site of the former Empire Lumber Company.

Picturesque Village

Empire, once a thriving lumber town, remains a picturesque village today. This postcard view, circa 1915, shows the Wilce home on the hill, with the Aylsworth Boarding House on the left and hardware store on the right. George Aylsworth, one of the early settlers of Empire, arrived in 1873 and built the first mill and dock. The boarding house served as quarters for his workers. In 1887 the T. Wilce Company formed the Empire Lumber Company to supply wood for its Chicago factory, which produced patented tongue and groove flooring. The Harvey Wilce bungalow was built in 1910 overlooking the Empire Lumber Company complex from its perch atop "Storm Hill."

Dealers in Everything

The Empire Lumber Company Store was built in 1888 to serve the growing population of Empire. The huge store was located on the southwest corner of Front Street at Lake Street, the present location of Deerings Food Market. Painted signs on the building advertised the stores services: "Dealers in Everything. Cash Paid for All Kinds of Forest Products. Choice Farming Lands for Sale Cheap." The building burned down about 1927.

Western Hotel

Originally built as the New European Hotel in 1894 by R.J. Middaugh, the hotel was renamed the Western Hotel in 1898 by its new owners. The fine building was located on the north side of Niagara at La Rue Street. The hotel's letterhead proclaimed it "an ideal place to enjoy your vacation. Located in the best fruit belt in Michigan." An early advertisement read, "A Good Eating House where Good Eaters get Good Eats." The hotel was torn down in 1935.

81

Modern Town

Empire was a vibrant community when M-22 came through the area. Many early photographs feature autos in front of local businesses, conveying the message that Empire was a "modern" town. Shown on the left is the John Fry store, circa 1910, which sold general merchandise.

In the photo below, the white building on the left was originally a millinery and jewelry shop, and subsequently used as a meat market owned by Deering and Payment at the time of this photo, circa 1920. It later served as the Empire Post Office until 1960. The brick building on the right was the Empire Exchange Bank.

Serving the Customer

Empire served the local villagers, lumbermen and farmers, as well as the summer vacationers, with well-stocked stores that met the diverse needs of their many customers. Over the years there were general stores, grocery stores, meat markets, hardware stores, clothing shops, shoe stores and others. There were also restaurants, taverns and ice-cream parlors. A few of the early businesses, like the Friendly Tavern and Deering's Market, have survived and prospered.

Postcard message:

Dear friend -
We are having hot weather here and I suppose it's the same there. But we have the big lake to swim in here and the breeze off the lake is cool. This little town of Empire is nice. Had some wonderful fresh strawberries yesterday.

-Marion

Postmarked Empire, 1950
Mailed to Battle Creek, Mich.

Empire, Mich.

Taghon's Corner

Charles and Louise Taghon came to Empire from Belgium in 1905. Charles found a job in the Empire Mill and Louise took in laundry from the Western Hotel. In 1923 the Taghons purchased a grocery store on the corner of Front Street and M-22. The building had been previously a print shop where The *Empire Journal* was published. In 1924 they opened a gas station in a small building behind the store selling Standard Oil (about where the Lakeshore Motel is now). The Taghons saw an opportunity to cater to the influx of visitors and working men in the area and expanded their home to include rooms for rent and a small restaurant. Mrs. Taghon offered a home-like atmosphere to men working on county roads, stringing telephone lines, installing electric lights, etc. With the success of this venture into the hospitality industry, the Taghons converted the grocery store into a tavern.

Taghon's Service Station

The small gas station built by Charles and Louise Taghon was later operated by their son, Fred, who then took over Al Verno's station. The original Verno building was disassembled in 1935 block by block from its location on Front Street (about where Deering's Market is now), and rebuilt on the southeast corner of M-22 and Front Street. In 1945 the station was sold to Fred Taghon, who expanded the business with Standard Oil products, automotive repairs and road service. In 1958 Fred opened Taghon's Gas Station across the street and turned the automotive repair side over to his son, Mike, who named the old station Taghon's Garage. When Mike retired in 1980, he turned the garage over to his son Dennis. When Fred retired in 1980, his son Dave Taghon along with Dave's wife Diane and family then ran the Amoco station converting it into an Amoco Food Shop in 1984. Dave's interest in history led him to create a replica of his grandparents' gas station inside the Amoco Food Shop, which was moved to the Empire Museum when Dave retired in 2002. Four generations of Taghons have left a distinctive mark on the community of Empire.

North Bar Lake Empire Mich o 15

North Bar Lake

North Bar Lake is located just north of Empire. The small lake of approximately 35 acres takes its name from how the lake was formed - ponded behind a sand bar. It is known to become dammed up when strong westerly storms drive waves and sand into its outlet. At other times, the outlet into Lake Michigan opens freely. North Bar Lake with its shallow, clear water and sandy bottom has long been a favorite swimming hole for locals and visitors alike.

The Fishing is excellent here.

Greetings from EMPIRE, MICH.

Lake Michigan Beach, Empire, Mich.

Postcard message:

Wed- Windy sunny day here. Went out to the big lake for swimming, but water was cold! Walked the beach and found 4 beautiful stones to bring back home. (Not me on the front of this postcard - ha ha.)

-Mel

Postmarked Empire, 1959
Mailed to Lansing, Mich.

On Lake Michigan Beach. Empire, Mich.

Soaring in the Dunes

"The soaring enthusiasts of the middle west have found the terrain in the dune country of Leelanau County near Sleeping Bear Dunes particularly suited to their activities and now take aloft with their man-made wings.... The broad smooth beach, the sheer face of the dune, rising 500 feet above the water, the prevailing westerly winds and the abundance of sunshine make for ideal flying conditions. Take-offs are made from the hard-packed beach. The gliders are attached behind a 'tow car' equipped with oversize tires which run over the surface of the sand at fifty or sixty miles an hour. The 'ships' rise rapidly above the speeding car at the end of an 800-foot cable, then cut loose, circle into the wind, and silently cruise above the dune, exploring the rising currents of air that shoot up from the face of the dune or rise in 'thermals' from the heated sand.

Often as many as six or eight of the ships are in the air at once, flying in formation or going off to explore new air currents. Always mindful of their ever-changing audience on the ground, there is one of the pilots whose job it is to land every fifteen or twenty minutes to show their guests just how the landings and take-offs are made....

Usually they are in the air shortly after dawn and darkness usually finds at least one of the ships still aloft so that fires have to be built on the beach to guide them to a safe landing as they come in."

-Preview of Your Complete Vacation in West Michigan, 1937

2nd Annual Mid-west GLIDER MEET

JUST NORTH OF

EMPIRE

ON SLEEPING BEAR DUNE

September 4 to 12 INCLUSIVE

Annual Gliding Contests

Annual gliding contests were held over the dunes just north of Empire on the shores of Lake Michigan. The first Midwest Open Soaring Meet was held on September 5-13, 1936. At the first meet the record for altitude was tied by four ships at a height of 1,550 feet. Total hours spent aloft by the ten ships were about 150 hours. The meets drew soaring enthusiasts from all over the country. Hundreds of spectators marveled at the motorless machines.

S.S. Puritan — Glen Haven Mich. — 23

Lake Traffic

The Michigan Transit Company steamers, *S.S. Manitou* and *S.S. Puritan*, docked in Glen Haven six times each week during the heyday of passenger steamships on the Great Lakes. When northbound they docked on Tuesday, Wednesday and Saturday; when southbound, it was on Thursday, Friday and Saturday. Vacationers and cottagers often took the overnight passage from Chicago and other ports and arrived the following morning in Glen Haven. Nearly all of the Lake Michigan traffic between Chicago and the Straits passed between the Manitou Islands and the mainland off Glen Haven.

Postcard message:

My dear little boy,
Don't this place look just right for lots of fun and all the nice clean sand there is around here to make mud pies and sand horses. Sometime you must come over here.

> *Much love & kisses, Aunt Dora*

Postmarked Glen Haven, 1920
Mailed to Milwaukee, Wis.

No. 12-4   Glen Haven Harbor from Sleeping Bear Dune, Michigan

U.S. Coast Guard

In 1901 the U.S. Life Saving Service built the Glen Haven station at Sleeping Bear Point. In 1915 the U.S. Life Saving Service was absorbed by the U.S. Coast Guard. In 1931 drifting sand and shoreline erosion forced the Sleeping Bear Point station to be moved to the present site in Glen Haven, one-half mile east of the original site. The boathouses and signal tower were also moved. Technological advances such as radios, radar and helicopters reduced the need for many Coast Guard stations. The Sleeping Bear Point station closed during World War II and stood idle until 1971, when it served for a short time as the visitor center for the newly-established Sleeping Bear Dunes National Lakeshore.

Surfmen

The Coast Guard surfmen often risked their lives rowing out on violent seas in open boats to rescue people from ships in distress. The boathouse at the Sleeping Bear Point station housed two surfboats, a fully-equipped beach cart, and other items needed to help in rescues. The tracks leading from the boathouse toward the lake assisted in launching the 26-foot boats. The men also had more mundane duties, such as practicing drills and manning the lookout tower. At night and on foggy days the surfmen would patrol the beach, lighting a Coston signal flare to alert ships that they had wandered too close to shore. Their constant vigilance prevented accidents and offered help when one did occur.

"SLEEPING BEAR INN"
Delightful Resort Hotel   Pleasantly Appointed
Excellently Cuisine   Rates Reasonable
GOLF, TENNIS AND HORSE BACK RIDING. SPECIAL AT-
TENTION GIVEN TO LUNCHEON, BRIDGE AND DINNER
PARTIES.

E. L. GALLAGHER, Mgr.

Sleeping Bear Inn — Glen Haven Mich 34

Sleeping Bear Inn

The Sleeping Bear Inn, originally named the Sleeping Bear House, was built in 1857 by C.C. McCarty, who also built a sawmill close by. The hotel served as a boarding house for mariners and lumberjacks working in the area, as well as overnight accommodations for passengers traveling by steamship. In 1878 the Northern Transit Company purchased the Inn and the surrounding properties in Glen Haven to assure a sufficient supply of wood for their fleet. In 1881 D.H. Day purchased the company's holdings in Glen Haven, including the Inn where he lived in a two-room suite until his marriage in 1889. During this time period the Inn was enlarged to accommodate more patrons. The rooms in the front of the building were nicer than the ones in the back and were rented to businessmen and travelers. Working men stayed in the bunk rooms at the back.

As the area began to draw more tourists, the hotel became more of a resort. In anticipation of the development of the Day Forest Estates, the Inn was renovated with the expectation of hosting wealthy investors in the project. Garages were built to house their automobiles and provide quarters for their chauffeurs. The large porch was enclosed in 1928 and dinner dances were held there for the guests. Bountiful home-cooked dinners were a specialty of the Inn. Louis and Marion Warnes purchased the Inn from the D.H. Day estate in 1937 and catered to summer tourists for 35 years. They closed the hotel in 1972, two years after the Sleeping Bear Dunes National Lakeshore was created. The Inn is now part of the Glen Haven Village Historic District, which is listed on the National Register of Historic Places.

D.H. Day of Glen Haven

"This is a region of Indian legend and scenic beauty. Glen Haven, lying between Pyramid Point and Sleeping Bear Point, was once a sawmill town and lumber shipping port. It was a regular port of call for passenger steamships. Here lived David H. Day. Old lumberman, pioneer in reforestation, a promoter of Western Michigan development, a leading actor in the drama of Lumbering Michigan who had a vision of the better, more enduring Recreational Michigan that was to follow."

-Stace, *Along Michigan's Coasts*, 1937

Locomotive - Day Lumber Mill

This locomotive hauled logs over a narrow-gauge track from D.H. Day's extensive timber holdings around Glen Lake to the Day saw mill in Glen Haven. The cut lumber was then loaded onto steamers and shipped to Chicago and other lake ports. At its peak, the mill produced up to 55,000 board feet of lumber a day and continued operation until 1923, well beyond the end of Michigan's lumber boom.

After Day's death, the Day estate loaned the locomotive to Clinch Park in 1939 for its lumber industry display. It was later sold to the Cedar Point amusement park, then moved to Greenfield Village, then acquired by the Port Huron Museum.

Locomotive, Day Lumber Mill, Glen Haven, Mich.

The D. H. Day Store
Glen Haven
L. C. Warnes, Proprietor
Quality Meats and Groceries
Also Ursa Vista Saddle Horses

Store and Post Office Glen Haven Mich.

D.H. Day Store

The D.H. Day General Store was the center of life in Glen Haven for several generations. The store was built in the 1870s after the dock and Sleeping Bear Inn were already established. The store was another of Day's entrepreneurial enterprises, along with his lumbering business and shipping concerns. The general store stocked items that lumbermen, fishermen, neighboring farmers, and local families might purchase. The store also served as the local post office, telegraph station, and ticket and freight office for boats docked at Glen Haven. The Day family lived above the store on the second floor. After Day's death the store was operated by Louis and Marion Warnes, Day's youngest daughter. It was the starting point for the Sleeping Bear Dunesmobile Rides from 1935 to 1978.

Glen Haven Canning Company

Workers at the Glen Haven Canning Company were guaranteed seasonal work during the busy harvest time. D.H. Day opened the state-of-the art cannery in 1923 and it continued to operate for twenty years. Day's own farm, Oswegatchie, as well as other farms in Leelanau County, produced cherries, peaches and apples, which were sent to the cannery. Fruit was also shipped from North Manitou Island to Glen Haven for processing. The canned fruit and juice were first shipped out of Glen Haven on lake boats such as the *SS Puritan*, but later shipped by truck. In a successful harvest year, over a million pounds of cherries were canned. The cannery building is now used by the National Park Service to display boats and related artifacts that interpret the story of the daily lives of mariners working in the area.

"OSWEGATCHIE" FARM GLEN HAVEN MICH.

Landmark Farm

"Oswegatchie" was D.H. Day's 400-acre farm, named after the area in New York state where Day's father was born. The barn, house and three outbuildings were built in the late 1880s and early 1890s. The outbuildings included a pig barn, a creamery, and a bull barn. The farm livestock included 200 Holsteins and 400 hogs. Day grew alfalfa, corn and hay. He also grew apples, cherries and peaches and had over 5,000 fruit trees in his orchards by the 1920s. Day was a proponent of scientific farming and was president of the West Michigan Development Bureau for many years. The beautiful farmhouse and barn located in the heart of the Sleeping Bear Dunes area have long been a favorite with photographers.

Guerrica Riding Stables

In the 1940s Bill Guerrica, an expert horseman of Spanish descent, operated a riding stable in the former D.H. Day barn on highway M-109. He offered guided tours on horseback in the dunes. Guerrica also worked with young men from Camp Leelanau for Boys in Glen Arbor. Some of his buckaroos are shown in this photo. In addition, Guerrica trailered horses from the Day barn to Crystalaire Camp for Girls on Crystal Lake, where he provided horseback riding instruction for the campers.

DAY FOREST ESTATES
ON
BEAUTIFUL GLEN LAKE
LEELANAU COUNTY, MICHIGAN
ESTATES IDEALLY RESTRICTED

APPLICATIONS FOR RESERVATIONS OF ESTATES NOW BEING RECEIVED

For particulars, write

J. B. WAGNER	B. R. HENDEL
General Manager	Sales Manager
Cadillac, Mich.	Manistee, Mich.

Day Forest Estates

In 1927 D.H. Day is shown holding a newspaper announcing the plans for the Day Forest Estates. In 1922 Day had sold a large portion of his land to a group of businessmen for a real estate development. Plans were drawn up for an exclusive resort on the 1,800-acre Alligator Hill, situated between Glen Lake and Lake Michigan. The project called for a magnificent golf clubhouse on the bluff, an eighteen-hole golf course, a beach and tennis club on the Lake Michigan shore, bridle paths, a polo field, an airstrip and a winter sports area. Facilities for swimming and boating were to be featured, including a rebuilt dock at Glen Arbor to accommodate yachts. Proposed were 120 estates, varying in size from five to thirty-five-acres, each with a marvelous view and "ideally restricted." Seven entrances were intended along with twelve miles of natural forest road. A proposal to make the Day Forest Estates the permanent summer home of the U.S. President was brought before a special session of Congress in 1928, but nothing came of idea. A major publicity campaign for the Day Forest Estates was underway when the stock market crashed in 1929, and plans for the development were halted. Only the golf course, several of the beautiful stone entrances, and a few miles of road were ever built. The Day Forest Estates did not prove to be a successful investment, but the predictions that values in the area would increase "by leaps and bounds" did prove true over the next several decades. Alligator Hill is now preserved as part of the Sleeping Bear Dunes National Lakeshore.

Gateway, Day Estates, Glen Lake, Mich.

Day Forest Golf Course

A golf course was one of the planned sites of the Day Forest Estates that actually was developed. An 18-hole course was built on Alligator Hill and opened about 1930. Broad and rolling fairways butted up against thick forest. Green fees were $1 a day with weekly and monthly rates available. The course closed in 1942, but evidence of the old fairways can still be seen on the Alligator Hill hiking trail, part of the Sleeping Bear Dunes National Lakeshore.

High Hill Lookout

"What was David H. Day's private forest on the high hill that stands between Lake Michigan and the crook in Glen Lake has been turned into a resort 'development.' A road leads up from M-109 near the Day State Park to an extraordinary lookout point at the top. The lookout faces the northwest. Off to the left is Sleeping Bear Point. Across the waters are the cliffs of South Manitou Island. Farther out is North Manitou. To the right is Pyramid Point. Along the shore is beating surf. In between shore and hill and up the hillside is heavy forest growth. The view is worth the climb."

-Stace, *Along Michigan's Coasts*, 1937

D.H. DAY STATE PARK IS LOCATED IN LEELANAU COUNTY, 6 MILES NORTH OF EMPIRE AND 2 MILES WEST OF GLEN ARBOR ON HIGHWAY M-109.

THE PARK CONSISTS OF 1,861 ACRES OF SAND DUNES WHICH IS ONE OF THE WORLD'S LARGEST SHIFTING SAND HILLS. OF ALL THE SAND DUNES ALONG THE PICTURESQUE MICHIGAN COASTLINE, SLEEPING BEAR IS THE FAVORITE. THIS NATURAL WONDER MICHIGANS "DESERT", HAS ONE ADVANTAGE OVER THE SAHARA — THE COOL, BOUNTIFUL AND BLUE WATERS OF LAKE MICHIGAN.

THE SLEEPING BEAR SAND DUNES ELEVATION 1044 FEET ABOVE SEA LEVEL, OFFERS UNLIMITED OPPORTUNITY FOR HIKING, EXPLORING, PHOTOGRAPHY, VIEWS OF ELEVATED SCENERY AND OCCASIONAL GLIMPSE OF THE USUAL NORTHERN WILDLIFE.

ENJOYABLE FOR PICNICING, CAMPING, FISHING, BOATING, SWIMMING, DUNE CLIMBING AND "THE DUNESMOBILE RIDE", AN EXCITING EXCURSION INTO STRANGE DESERT LAND. CARS LEAVE GLEN HAVEN AT FREQUENT INTERVALS FOR A COMPLETE TOUR OF THE DUNES WHICH IS UNDER SUPERVISION OF THE MICHIGAN DEPARTMENT OF CONSERVATION.

NATIVE WILD FLOWERS SCATTERED THROUGHOUT THE PARK AREA INCLUDE VIOLETS, ASTERS, TRILLIUM, ARBUTUS, WILD ROSE, BLUE EYED GRASS, TIGER LILY, SWEET PEA, MOCCASIN FLOWER, SAND CHERRIES AND INDIAN PETUNIA.

ADDITIONAL ATTRACTIONS - MEMORIAL MARKER COMMEMORATING MICHIGANS OLDEST STATE PARK; LOOKOUT TOWER OVERLOOKING LAKE MICHIGAN; NORTH & SOUTH MANITOU ISLANDS AND SURROUNDING AREAS; UNUSAL JUNIPER GROWTH; GLEN LAKES WITH THEIR VARIED COLORINGS, DRIVE-OUT LOOK-OUTS ON BORDERING HILLS AND A GREAT VARIETY OF BIRDS.

D.H. Day State Park

In 1919 the Michigan State Park Commission was established and D.H. Day was named chairman. His first act as chairman was to donate 32 sandy acres near Glen Haven. The acreage encompassed of 708 feet of unspoiled shoreline on Lake Michigan, creeping sand dunes and dense growths of juniper and pine. Day pointed out that this property was only a quarter of a mile from M-22, and offered to furnish funds to build a road from the highway to the new park. Although property for parks on Mackinac Island and at Interlochen was given to the State before the D.H. Day State Park was created in 1920, it was the first park set up under the new State Park Commission. By 1921 when the state parks were transferred to the Conservation Department, over twenty other sites had been acquired. The D.H. Day State Park became part of the Sleeping Bear Dunes National Lakeshore in 1975.

Caretaker's Home, State Park, Glen Haven, Mich.

Rustic Kitchen, State Park, Glen Haven, Mich.

Park Amenities

The D.H. Day State Park provided simple amenities for campers. Tent sites, well water, outhouses, picnic tables and bath houses were supplied for the campers' convenience. A log cabin offered shelter and a gathering place for visitors. Basic supplies such as bread and milk were available at a small store in the caretaker's house. A rustic kitchen with a cooking stove provided shelter while preparing meals. Playground equipment was erected for children. The fine bathing beach was a big attraction. Hiking through the surrounding woods and along the shore was a favorite pastime then as it still is today. A Michigan historical marker in front of the log cabin gives the history of Michigan's early state parks.

Timber Preserve

"The park is [located in] the famous second growth timber preserve planted years ago by David H. Day, who started life as a clerk on the dock at Glen Haven, became a man of wealth and one of the most public spirited boosters western Michigan has had. His private forest was an individual attempt of reforestation and shows what can be accomplished along this line in the life of one man."

-*Grand Rapids Press*, June 13, 1924

Postcard message:

July 2, 1928
Dear Mother,
Well here we are in the State Park - Glen Haven.
Our tent is right near the picture on the card. It
sure is nice here and how I wish you were with
us. Bert is sleeping now, had his dinner and laid
down and went to sleep. We sure have had a
fine trip so far. Had fish for dinner. We are over
300 miles from you. Will send another card.
                                                        -Nettie

Postmarked: Glen Haven, 1928
Mailed to Charlotte, Mich.

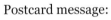
Bathing Beach
Michigan State Park No1
Glen Haven, Mich.

The Slide, Children's Play Ground, State Park, Glen Haven, Mich.

Postcard message:

D.H. Day State Park
June 20, 1938
Dear Mr. and Mrs. S.,
Having a nice time on vacation. Camped at this
beautiful park, caught lots of fish and go bathing
in Lake Michigan quite often. Have taken trips to
Northport Point, Crystal Lake and have visited
Traverse City several times. Was there for the
Cherry Festival, had a great time. Wish you were
all here to enjoy the fine fishing with us.
Best Regards to all, Emma and Harry

Postmarked Glen Arbor, 1938
Mailed to Detroit, Mich.

Bath Houses,
Michigan State Park #1
Glen Haven, Mich.

SLEEPING BEAR SAND DUNES, LAKE MICHIGAN AND EMPIRE BLUFFS IN THE DISTANCE—46

SLEEPING BEAR DUNES MICHIGAN

"Awesome, Amazing Sleeping Bear

Great bluffs rising 450 feet or more from the water's edge and extending two miles along the shore furnish an awesome sight for passengers and crews of boats sailing out of the Manitou Passage into the open reaches of Lake Michigan. Atop the bluffs is perched a sand dune 100 feet high. The dune is shaped - if one uses a little imagination - like a bear lying on its side. The dune is Sleeping Bear, thus named by the Indians in the long ago. The side toward the land is covered with an old forest; the side toward the lake is exposed sand.

While one particular perched dune is the actual Sleeping Bear, the name is applied to the whole amazing, blowing sand region. This region includes the Sleeping Bear plateau, a wind-swept desert tableland high above the big lake; the Sleeping Bear dune complex - as the geologists call it - and Sleeping Bear Point....

The sands, drifting over the east side of the plateau, have built up steep lee slopes of sand extending out a half mile or more from the original morainic ridge.... Upon the plateau itself is a perched dune complex, serving as a companion to Sleeping Bear....

North of the plateau the moraine drops to a plain reaching out to Sleeping Bear Point. Upon slopes and plain, sands blowing from the moraine have built up a mass of dunes - dune ridges, fixed dunes - covering an area a mile or so square....

The active dunes at the north end of the 'complex' are creeping eastward, carrying great masses of sand into Sleeping Bear Bay. The geologists say the eastern part of Glen Lake was once a bay that opened to the north into Lake Algonquin. A bar cut it off from the big lake. That bar remains as a sand ridge between Glen Lake and Sleeping Bear Bay."

-Stace, *Michigan Mystic Dunes*, 1939

The Legend of Sleeping Bear

"Native Ottawa and Chippewa tribesmen were impressed with the grandeur of the great dune now known as Sleeping Bear long before the white men came. Ages ago - the story goes - a black bear and her two cubs started to swim from Wisconsin to Michigan. When almost to shore the cubs became tired and lagged behind. The mother bear climbed to the top of the dune to wait for her babes, who never arrived. She still maintains her vigil, a great heap of dark colored vegetation atop the golden sands, while off shore the cubs have changed into islands, the North and South Manitous, mysterious and alluring in the distance."

-*Sleeping Bear Dunesmobile Scenic Dune Rides*, circa 1956

Buried Forest

"Sleeping Bear...contains several sections of forest exposed by the winds after years of burial, and gleaming in the sunlight like a cluster of bones. Wiry beach grass manages to maintain a precarious foothold on the dunes. Botanists and geologists find it a source of wonders. Snow and ice cover from the early Spring often remain a few feet beneath the sandy floor until late summer."

-*Detroit News*, August 29, 1948

Sand Ripples, Sleeping Bear Sand Dune, Glen Haven, Mich.

Fine Sand

"The sands ... are being moved by the west winds toward Glen Lake at the rate of six feet a year, burying trees and grass on nearby farms. An estimated 200 acres of sand at Sleeping Bear Point, chiseled by the wind and undermined by the lake currents, vanished into Lake Michigan in 1915. So fine is the sand that some parts of the dune are suitable for summer sand-dune skiing. Prevailing westerly winds make it an ideal place for glider take-offs."

-*Michigan: A Guide to the Wolverine State*, 1941

Natural Wonder

"At Glen Haven, towering above Lake Michigan, is the Sleeping Bear, the largest traveling sand dune in the world. This mysterious, shifting mountain of sand is one of Michigan's most dramatic natural wonders. A growth of dark conifers along its ridge gives it the appearance of a recumbent bear and the name, Sleeping Bear."

-Grand Traverse Bay Region - Michigan's Sunshine Corner, 1944

A Pinnacle of Sand Sleeping Bear Glen Haven Mich

A View From The Sand Dunes. Glen Haven Mich W48

Postcard message:

Great "Sleeping Bear" sand dune over 400 ft. in height. Spreads far out. All of these sand dunes really a chain, comes out of Lake Mich. Even vegetation grows on this sand.

Postcard not mailed.

Dune Climb

For generations, thousands of people have scaled the Dune Climb as an annual tradition when visiting Sleeping Bear Dunes. For years the Dune Climb was known locally as the "Toboggan Slide." The Dune Climb is about 130 feet high to the top of the first dune, and then another 130 feet to the top of the second dune. The angle of the slope is slightly less than 20 degrees. At the crest of the first dune Little Glen Lake comes into view. At the top of the second dune a more impressive view appears, but Lake Michigan does not come into view until one makes a strenuous one and a half mile hike over five more dunes. The terrain of the dunes can be a curious sight with ripples of sand, deep blow-outs and ghost forests. The Dune Climb is an active moving sand dune, creeping towards the parking lot at a rate of about three feet a year. In the last forty years, the parking lot has been moved back twice.

TOBOGGAN SLIDE at GLEN LAKE   C2889

Photographer's Wonderland

The Sleeping Bear Dunes are truly a
photographer's dream. The stark landscape,
rippled sand, barren trees, majestic dunes,
and crashing waves are fitting subjects for any
photographer. One of the most dramatic scenes
often captured by camera is the shore looking
north towards the Sleeping Bear Dune from
Empire Bluffs.

Horseback Riding

Horseback excursions into the Sleeping Bear Dunes gave riders a chance to experience the dunes "up close and personal." Louis and Marion Warnes offered horseback riding in the 1930s before they started the dunesmobile rides. Bill Guerrica, a "genuine horseman of the West," led trips across the dunes in the 1940s for the general public and as well as his students at Camp Leelanau for Boys. Girls from Camp Kohahna were led across the dunes on horseback by Lucille Baker Barratt. These trips took riders through deep forest, along the shore of Lake Michigan and over the dunes. Carrying riders in the hot sun and sand was hard on the horses and was discontinued as more people began choosing to see the dunes from a dunesmobile than on horseback.

Skiing on the Dunes

"If you want to try the comparatively new sport of summer skiing, bring along your equipment. With a steep sand dune, your bathing suit, and a pair of skis, you can put in a novel afternoon skiing down the sand. It is much slower than snow skiing but with a proper pitch, you can get about as much speed as you want unless you are an expert."

-*Mc Cracken's 1940 Guide to Michigan*

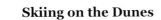

111

Dunesmobiles

In the mid-1930s Louis Warnes was riding his horse over the hot sand of Sleeping Bear Dunes. The view from the crest of the dunes was breathtaking and he reasoned to himself that there must be a way to share this splendor with the public. The few horses he rented were overworked because of the rugged terrain, hot sand and high demand for their services. He bought a used 1934 Ford convertible and found a set of balloon tires with wide surface treads and low air pressure. Warnes mapped out a 13-mile trail over the dunes, and in 1935 started the dune rides. The first dunesmobile took four people at a cost of 25 cents each. By 1942 eight more dunesmobiles had been added to the caravan including a 1935 Ford, four 1937 Fords, two 1939 Fords and a 1941 Mercury. Then after WWII, ten 1948 Ford convertibles were purchased to replace the aging fleet. Later came ten 1956 red and white Oldsmobile convertibles, ordered without the optional heaters or radios. The 1964 red Ford dunes wagons were the last fleet of dunesmobiles. The rides were discontinued in 1978 under an agreement with the Sleeping Bear Dunes National Lakeshore to protect the fragile ecosystem of the sand dunes.

AT THE FOOT OF THE DUNES GLEN LAKE

Scenic Sand Dune Rides

"I rode with Louis Warnes
*   O'er the crest of Sleeping Bear,*
And I viewed the scenic beauty
*   That is quite beyond compare.*

For a trip by 'special' auto
*   Up this mighty dune of sand,*
Holds a thrill that can't be equalled
*   In this wondrous Northern Land.*

Now I guess I'll have to leave you,
*   For I've time to write no more,*
But 'The Caravan' is waiting
*   in Glen Haven by the store."*

-postcard advertisement attributed
to Marion and Louis Warnes, circa 1938

Sleeping Bear
Scenic Sand Dune Rides
Glen Haven
The Great Moving Desert
of Northern Michigan
Overlooking Glen Lake and Lake Michigan
For reservations phone or write
Louis C. Warnes
"The Original Sand Dune Ride"

CAR USED ON SAND DUNES NEAR GLEN LAKE - MICH

Wide Balloon Tires

"Automobiles that negotiate sand dunes present a different type of tire problem than those used on highways.... Entrepreneur Warnes turned to ... 9.00-16 Goodyear All-Weather Tread Air-Wheels, air pressure in which is about 12 pounds, and which give the cars a broad, secure underfooting, with plenty of traction, and no tendency to become sanded in, or bogged down."

-*The Good Year News*, October 1940

Finding Snow

"Finding Snow on West Michigan Desert - In these days when the temperature on the Sleeping Bear sand dunes in Leelanau County usually is at summer pitch, these girls find snow and ice. The snow, about three feet under the surface of the shifting sand, was discovered by Louis C. Warnes of Glen Haven, who operates a fleet of motorcars that carry tourists on a 13-mile ride over the dunes. It was explained by Warnes that the shifting sands cover the snow in early spring, and even in late summer, it is possible to find snow along the Lake Michigan beach."

-Grand Rapids Press, July 22, 1947

1948 Dunesmobiles

"One of the chief attractions of 'The Bear' is a hell-for-leather ride over the steep dunes in one of the dunesmobiles operated by Louis C. Warnes and his wife, Marion, who also run the Sleeping Bear Inn and a souvenir shop in tiny Glen Haven.

The [1948] dunesmobile isn't a great deal different from a stock model V-8. The most outstanding feature is the big 9 x 13 air wheel that replaces the standard tire. Carrying only 15 pounds of air, the doughnut tires spread out to a tread of 11 inches, supporting the dunesmobile snowshoe-like. They are equipped with mountain gears (actually the back axle of a Ford pick-up) for more rapid acceleration and better pulling power, and heavy station wagon springs are used. The final alteration is to replace the exhaust muffler with a straight pipe....

The cars reach 50 to 60 m.p.h. over the mounds of fine sand. The 13-mile dune route starts at Glen Haven, where State Highway 209 runs into Lake Michigan. Despite warning signs, tourists frequently try to drive their big sedans over the dunes, but become hopelessly bogged."

-Ford Times, April 1948

Outstanding Scenic Views

"Trips over the dunes in specially-built motorcars are offered at Glen Haven. This is a scenic ride into the desert-like hills, where forests of Michigan's early days are buried by the constantly moving sands. One of the most outstanding scenic views in America is from the brim of the dunes across the vast expanse of blue water that is Glen Lake, framed in the splendor of Michigan's pine forests. The dunes are one of Michigan's unspoiled naturally scenic sections."

-Carefree Days in West Michigan, 1950

Michigan's Sahara

"Automotive science, which produced tanks that surmounted all sorts of obstacles in World War II, has conquered the biggest shifting sand dune in America - Sleeping Bear Point.... The great dune is a miniature version of the Sahara desert, seven and a half miles long and more than two miles wide. Here and there vegetation occurs in wiry tufts of beach grass and stunted trees struggling valiantly for life against the onslaught of sand creeping inland at the rate of six feet a year....

Where the family automobile would bury itself to the running board, a specially engineered 'dunesmobile' proceeds at a cruising speed of 35 miles per hour.... From 12,000 to 15,000 persons annually roll over the Bear, as it is known to natives, from the store of Louis C. Warnes, of Glen Haven. Warnes operates a fleet of unique automobiles. Although the dune is the property of the State Conservation Department, Warnes enjoys exclusive automotive travel rights inasmuch as he owns the approaches."

-Detroit News, August 29, 1948

117

New 1956 Fleet

Proud employees of the Frank G. Paulos Oldsmobile dealership in Traverse City pose with the new fleet of 1956 Oldsmobile Super 88 convertibles. The cars were fitted with wide balloon tires, but had no heat or radios. They stand ready for delivery to Louis C. Warnes of Sleeping Bear Dunesmobile Scenic Dune Rides.

Great Tourist Attraction

"The vast desert-like expanse is a great tourist attraction. Specially-built deluxe motorcars carry visitors over the sands, to the 'Sleeping Bear' for a view across the Lake Michigan waters toward the Manitou Islands, then on to other vantage points where the vista thrills those getting their first sight of Glen Lake.... The fleet of Dunesmobiles operate daily from Glen Haven at the end of Highway M-109."

-*Carefree Days in West Michigan*, 1956

One of Summer's Great Experiences

"Sleeping Bear is the world's largest traveling sand dune, towering over the blue waters of Lake Michigan on one side and above Glen Lake on the other. One of summer's great experiences is a ride up and down the almost perpendicular face of the dunes on a dunesmobile. It is breathtaking."

-*Vacation Days in Michigan's Grand Traverse Bay Region*, 1960

Safe and Comfortable

"... A fleet of safe, comfortable new Super
88 Oldsmobile convertibles is kept busy
each day from the latter part of May until
Oct 1st.... Cars leave at frequent intervals
from the Sleeping Bear Gift Shop at
Glen Haven, located on M-209 on Lake
Michigan. The 'dunesmobile' ride is the
only complete tour of the dunes and is
operated under lease and supervision of
the Michigan Conservation Department."

*-Sleeping Bear Dunesmobile
Scenic Dune Rides,* circa 1959

Louis Warnes

Louis C. Warnes, seen below, is proudly standing next to one of his 1956 dunesmobiles. Warnes and his wife, Marion, operated the scenic dunesmobile rides for over 40 years, providing thousands of visitors with rides over the dunes in style and comfort.

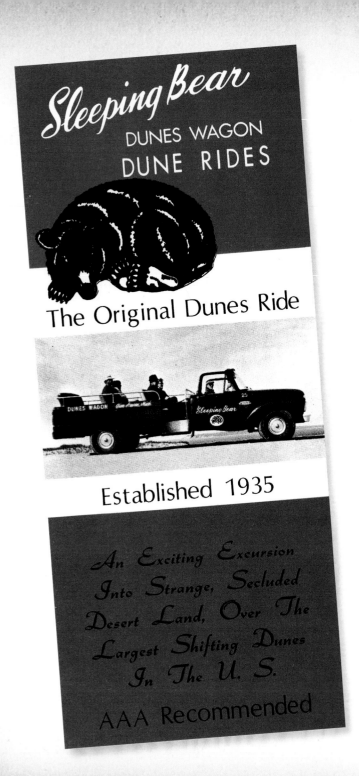

Note on back of photo:

August 11 & 12, 1967
Had a great trip! Climbed the sand dunes on Fri. - even Mom - and Blake loved all that sand! Also took the "Dune wagon" ride out in the "Sleeping Bear" dunes - lots of fun! On Sat. we took a canoe trip down the Platte River to Lake Michigan and that was beautiful too. Camped at D.H. Day State Park. Nice weather.

Dunes Wagon Dune Rides

"Exciting automobile excursion into a strange, secluded desert land set between beautiful Glen Lake and Lake Michigan. Nowhere is there an experience exactly like these dune rides. It is a brief safari into the African desert without the heat. It is a 19 square mile expanse of unspoiled and untamable natural beauty, where views are spectacles of rare beauty and Lake Michigan is majestic in its every mood. All vehicles are custom built and have over-size sand tires. The guides are competent and courteous and can answer your questions about the Dunes and surrounding area.... The Dunes Wagon ride is the only complete tour of the dunes and is operated under lease and supervision of the Sleeping Bear Dunes National Lakeshore."

-Sleeping Bear Dunes Wagon Dune Rides, circa 1972

A Sleeping Bear State Park?

By the mid-1920s the Sleeping Bear region was getting throngs of tourists along M-22, and both Benzie State Park and D.H. Day State Park were often filled to capacity with campers. In 1941 the citizens of Benzie County lobbied the Michigan Department of Conservation to expand their small state park of 180 acres, or create a new state park in the dune country between Point Betsie and the west end of Crystal Lake. At the same time Leelanau County also coveted a new state park.

The Department of Conservation agreed to survey the entire length of the Lake Michigan shoreline between Frankfort and Leland for potential parklands. The survey recommended that if the state were to have only one new state park in Benzie or Leelanau County, it should be in the vicinity of Glen Lake and the Sleeping Bear Dunes. Specifically, the potential park would encompass the dunes, the Day Forest Estates, and 1,000 feet of the north shore of Glen Lake, for a total of 5,800 acres. Although the report was well received in Lansing, WWII stopped any further expansion of parkland.

The idea for a Sleeping Bear state park was revisited in 1946, and negotiations began to acquire the failed Day Forest Estates property, but stalled because pressure by the Michigan Conservation Commission to increase funding for site development and maintenance of the current parks prevented its support of any further land acquisitions. In 1949 there was an effort by Glen Lake area residents to purchase the lakefront property along Lake Michigan and Glen Lake. The residents then proposed that the State secure the forested lands inland. This plan failed to find legislative or Conservation Department approval. A final attempt to raise funds to purchase the land outright only confirmed commitments for $60,000, which was not enough, and when the Glen Lake residents' option expired, the plan was relinquished.

Previously, in 1931, the Michigan Department of Conservation had acquired from the federal government 1,545 acres of Sleeping Bear duneland to the west of Day Forest Estates. Further acquisitions were acquired by gifts and Fish and Game funds. These existing state lands had been consolidated under the state park administration, but there still remained a considerable amount of private property within the proposed area for the new state park. By 1963 the State owned only 2,044 acres of the proposed 5,800 acres. The realization of a park in the Sleeping Bear Dunes and Glen Lake region had to wait until the creation of the Sleeping Bear Dunes National Lakeshore.

1,400-Acre Privately-Owned Park

Since the 1930s there had been talk of establishing a state park in the Sleeping Bear Dunes area, and some serious efforts had been made. In 1961 a proposal was made for a national park. But neither the state nor the federal government were able to raise enough support to make the park a reality.

Pierce Stocking, a local lumberman and landowner, was frustrated by government stagnation on creating a park and decided to open one himself, promising to preserve the area's natural beauty. In 1967 Stocking announced plans for a privately-developed park in the heart of the Sleeping Bear Dunes proposed national lakeshore, including the duneland located between the west end of Little Glen Lake and Lake Michigan. The area known as Day Forest Estates and other land owned by Stocking was not included in his new dunes park.

The Sleeping Bear Dunes Park opened in 1968 with a scenic drive, picnic area, restrooms, park headquarters and parking lot. The private park included a forest of mixed hardwoods, hilly terrain and a number of scenic overlooks. When the National Park Service team visited the park, they gave a "favorable response." But the commercial park was a reminder that the fate of the dunes remained partly in private hands. After the private park was absorbed into the National Lakeshore, the scenic drive was enlarged and fittingly named after Pierce Stocking, shown in the photo.

"Welcome to a Beautiful New Recreation Area

From the most beautiful section of America's most splendorous state comes a hearty welcome to every member of your family. In the very heart of this lovely, unspoiled area, the 1,400-acre Sleeping Bear Dunes Park has been privately developed as a family recreation center, preserving its natural charm for the enjoyment of people of all ages. The park is a realization of a dream of preserving for future generations a portion of Michigan's near-primeval forest lands to which they might turn as a haven of rest after struggling with our highly developed, technically-modern world.

Situated in one of the most attractive regions in our nation, Sleeping Bear Dunes Park is lavishly forested with towering trees and all-but-dominated by strangely beautiful sand dunes."

-Sleeping Bear Dunes Park, circa 1968

LAKESHORE OR EYESORE? SAVE SLEEPING BEAR DUNES

SLEEPING BEAR TASK FORCE, P.O. 2085, ANN ARBOR, MICHIGAN, 48106

NATIONAL PARK

U.S. Senator Philip A. Hart, shown here at a National Parks event, ranked his role in creating the Sleeping Bear Dunes National Lakeshore as one of his proudest accomplishments.

Creation of the National Lakeshore

In 1957 and 1958 the National Park Service conducted surveys of possible locations for new parks, concluding that there were only a few remaining large stretches along the entire Great Lakes shore that might still be protected from further development. Sleeping Bear Dunes was identified as an area of "national significance" and one of the most important areas worthy of preservation.

In 1961 U.S. Senator Philip A. Hart proposed a bill creating a national park in the Sleeping Bear Dunes area. Hart faced a battle with local landowners, who fought for their property rights. Local governmental units were afraid of a significant tax base loss. Some opponents simply didn't trust the government and thought that mixing private commercial enterprises, farming and recreation with public land wouldn't work. Others said that there were enough parks in the area, and a large national park was not needed. It didn't help that the federal government advocated letting the land go back to nature, which would involve razing many houses and cottages, in an area that had not been a wilderness for over a hundred years. Some people living in the area felt that they were good stewards of the land and did not want it to be overwhelmed by tourists.

But Hart would not let Sleeping Bear lie. He had strong citizen support throughout the state, and help from national groups such as the Sierra Club and the National Wildlife Federation. The environmental movement was bringing a new awareness to the public of the fragile dune and forest ecosystems. Hart had backing from Rep. James O'Hara, a Utica Democrat, and Rep. Guy Vander Jagt, a Cadillac Republication, in whose district the proposed park would be located. To address the concerns of the opposition, compromises were made. Park boundaries were redrawn to exclude most of the property around Platte and Glen Lakes. People within the proposed boundaries who had built on their property before 1965 were allowed to keep their homes. The Michigan legislature appropriated some tax relief money for local schools in the dunes area.

On October 21, 1970 President Nixon signed Public Law 91-479 creating the Sleeping Bear Dunes National Lakeshore. Eventually people in the area accepted that the National Park Service was a good steward of the land and that the National Lakeshore was good for the region. In honor of Phil Hart's persistent efforts in saving the Sleeping Bear Dunes, the visitors' center carries his name. In 2014, 32,500 acres were formally designated as wilderness within the Sleeping Bear Dunes National Lakeshore.

Dedication of the Sleeping Bear Dunes National Lakeshore

The Sleeping Bear National Lakeshore was formally dedicated on October 22, 1977, exactly seven years and one day after Congress passed legislation creating the park. "The Sleeping Bear Dunes are one of the wonders of our state and nation." With those words, Governor William G. Milliken dedicated the 71,000-acre national lakeshore. Milliken paid tribute to the late Senator Philip A. Hart, for his personal commitment to the establishment of the National Lakeshore despite the many obstacles and prolonged disagreements between government officials and local landowners. Milliken stated, "the preservation of this area represents a legacy of Phil Hart to the people he served."

Milliken also cited three other persons who were key players in preserving the dunes: Harold Titus of Traverse City, who as chairman of the Michigan Conservation Commission in 1946, brought the area to state attention; Carl T. Johnson of Cadillac, who was the former chairman of the Michigan Natural Resources Commission, and Genevieve Gillette, conservationist, citizen activist and well-known parks-proponent.

Speeches from local, state and National Park Service dignitaries were flavored with reminiscences of the battles fought for the preservation of the area. First-hand recollections were delivered by Julius Martinek of Frankfort, the first superintendent of the lakeshore park. The ceremonies, attended by several hundred people, took place at the foot of the Sleeping Bear Dune Climb.

Most Beautiful Lake

Glen Lake's reputation for beauty goes back many years. In fact, it was well established long before Good Morning America's designation in 2012 as "the most beautiful place in America" brought the Sleeping Bear Dunes region to the country's attention. A 1926 article in the *Traverse City Record Eagle* quoted Professor Laphan of Columbia University as saying in his column for *National Geographic* magazine that "Glen Lake is one of the five most beautiful lakes in the world." Although this quotation has never been substantiated, it has taken on a life of its own. Variations have appeared over the years. Glen Lake has been called "the most beautiful lake in the nation"; "the second most beautiful lake in the world"; and the "third most beautiful lake in the world." The Glen Lake region has also been called the "Little Switzerland of America" and the "Como of America."

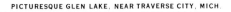

Greetings from GLEN LAKE, MICH.

M-22 at Glen Lake

"M-22 winds south from Burdickville at the east end of Glen Lake to Empire. Glen Lake is in a class by itself.... [It] need yield its place to no other in Michigan, if not the whole country, for beauty.... The lake proper is almost perfectly circular, while the west end which is separated by a bridge at 'The Narrows,' is almost another lake."

-Grand Rapids Herald, August 14, 1927

M-22 ON GLEN LAKE, MICH. L-1817

21529

GLEN LAKE TRAILER CAMP
On M-22, 4½ Miles North of Empire, Mich.

Glen Lake Trailer Camp

VOLNEY DORSEY, Proprietor

Good Boats, Fine Bathing Beach, Excellent Fishing Grounds
Good Water — Electricity — Toilets
One Third Mile West of Glen Lake Bridge on M-22

Postcard message:

Hi, Got here about 3:30 am Sunday - it is simply beautiful. The girls are having a wonderful time and so are we. The trailer court had a chicken BBQ tonight, about 100 people were there. So far we have had nice weather.

Love, Joyce

Postmarked Empire, 1951
Mailed to Bluffton, Indiana

M22 At The Book Nook
Glen Lake N7

Tobin's Corner

The intersection of M-22 and the Glen Lake Narrows bridge was a busy spot. The area was once known as Glenmere and even had its own post office from 1905 until 1916. Several businesses operated at this corner over the years including Tobins Store, the Book Nook, and Karen's Gift Shop.

Richard Tobin operated a store and lunch room just south of the Narrows bridge on the south side of Glen Lake. Catering to the growing number of motorists exploring the area, he started selling Red Crown gasoline, but later switched to Sinclair gas.

Tobin's Store, Glen Lake, Mich.

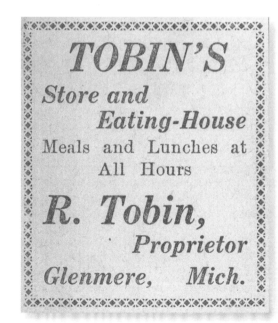

TOBIN'S
Store and
Eating-House
Meals and Lunches at All Hours

R. Tobin,
Proprietor
Glenmere, Mich.

Postcard message:

Had a dandy trip up here. Have a nice cottage on Glen Lake. Expect to stay here till Thurs then go to Lake Leelanau til Sat. Men caught dandy perch and bass this morn. Are going to the Dunes now. This sure is a beautiful Lake. Wish you were here.

-Vivian

Postmarked Empire, 1943
Mailed to Grand Rapids, Mich.

Narrows Bridge, Glen Lake, Michigan.

The Narrows Bridge

The Glen Lake Narrows was first crossed by a wooden bridge built in 1871. The second bridge, constructed of iron and wood, was completed in 1905. It was at this point that people began to refer to "Big Glen" and "Little Glen." Construction began in 1928 on the third bridge to cross the Narrows on M-22. This new concrete bridge proved defective and had to be rebuilt. It was completed in 1930, much to the delight of motorists who had been making the long detour around Glen Lake. In 2006 the bridge was designated the memorial "Carl Oleson Jr. Bridge." Oleson was an avid fisherman and the long-time owner of the Sportsman Shop in Glen Arbor. When the current bridge was built in 2009, the memorial designation remained.

Postcard message:

Dear Mrs. D.J. and family,
We have a cabin on Glen Lake for a week. The lake is beautiful but the fishing not too good. We were fortunate in finding a woman who bakes bread and pies near here. Her baking is fine although her bread is white instead of dark. Have a nice cherry pie for dinner. Our cabin has a screened in porch overlooking the lake.

Sincerely, Beryl

Postmarked Empire, 1928
Mailed to Kalamazoo, Mich.

Postcard message:

The weather has been lovely. We are enjoying driving around and the scenery is lovely. We are at a place called Dunn's Farm on a beautiful lake. We eat in the dining room and the maids keep our place clean, so all we have to do is eat, sleep and play. This is real rest. Will tell you more about it when I get home.

-Anna

Postmarked Traverse City, 1930
Mailed to Cooperstown, New York

Postcard message:

Hello Sis, - How are you all; we are having the time of our lives. Tell Lonie I caught a Pickerel 23 inches long, weighs 3 lbs. We are in a nice place about 3 miles from this scene. We will be home Sunday.

-Karen

Postmarked Glen Arbor, 1939
Mailed to Bairdstown, Ohio

Carr's Boat House and Lodge on M-22, Glen Lake, Mich.

Carr's Resort

Carr's Resort on M-22 at the Glen Lake Narrows got its start as Carr's Cabin Camps in the late 1920s. The housekeeping cabins had electric lights and running water. A unique feature of the cabins was an attached garage, which was a great convenience to overnight guests with open automobiles. It also offered privacy for the autos of some salacious persons for whom privacy was paramount.

Carr's soon build a tourist lodge and boathouse to accommodate the growing number of vacationers and fishermen coming to Glen Lake in the 1930s. The resort was known for its Sunday chicken dinners and "home-cooked popular-priced meals." A grocery store, operated in connection with Carr's, offered home-baked goods. The resort advertised that boating, bathing and fishing amenities were "but a step from the front door."

Postcard message:

Dear Ruth -
It is rather cool here but we sure had a good rest in this cabin. X is where we stayed. Sure seems funny not to have you with us. We will come up here again sometime. I hope you are well and I expect to see you soon. Dad is enjoying his vacation but he is lonesome without you along.

-Mother

Postmarked: Lake Leelanau, 1931
Mailed to Grand Rapids, Mich.

Mac Donald's Resort   Glen Lake Mich.   C-2717

Mac Donald's
(formerly Carr's Resort)

Evan Mac Donald purchased Carr's Resort in 1935. Proud of Glen Lake's reputation as "the most beautiful lake in the nation," MacDonald welcomed vacationers to his lodge, which was "but a few steps from the water's edge." The several apartments available for rent were furnished in a "comfortable, homelike manner suitable to sportsmen." Mac Donald's boat livery, one of the largest in the area, was equipped with outboard motors, rowboats, motorboats, and pleasure boats for those seeking relaxation on the crystal water or a chance to try their rod on the lake's bass, perch and pickerel. Minnows and bait were also supplied for the eager fishermen.

EDGEWATER RESORT   GLEN LAKE   C 2791

Edgewater Resort

Howard's Edgewater Resort was one of the many cottage colonies dotting the shores of Glen Lake in the 1930s and 1940s. It offered cabins and cottages for rent on the west side of Big Glen, north of the Narrows. A small store sold Cities Service gasoline, Coca-Cola and other items to vacationers in the area.

Postcard message:

Dear Mother,
We are now at the second most
beautiful lake in the world according
to the National Geographic Society
and here we intend to stay.

-Tom

Postmarked Glen Arbor, 1936
Mailed to Saginaw, Mich.

HOWARDS EDGEWATER RESORT - GLEN LAKE Mich.

Ray's Resort

Ray's Resort was located close to the Narrows on the southwest shore of Glen Lake. It was built by Welby C. Ray, probably about 1900. In 1922 the resort was turned over to Ray's son, Max Milton and his wife, Nellie. The white farmhouse-style building had a wraparound porch on two sides, making for comfortable lounging space for guests to catch the cool breezes off the lake. Shuffleboard and horseshoes were available for guests. Glen Lake offered ample boating, fishing and swimming recreation. Accommodations were provided with five bedrooms and two baths. Several rental cottages were located on the property. In the early 1930s the management was turned over to Mrs. I. Eastman who built the resort's reputation for fine food. Ray's Resort offered "dinners for tourists," specializing in fish and chicken meals. Lunches were available at all hours. The resort was sold in the mid-1940s to William Gross, and became known as the Glen Lodge. In the 1970s it became a private home and was razed in 1993.

Ray's Resort, Glen Lake, Michigan.

Shore Line at Ray's Resort, Glen Lake, Mich.

Postcard message:

Dear Merle,
We are staying at Glen Lake near Traverse City. We were out in a launch today on Glen Lake and went from that into two little lakes. It is beautiful here like some great big picture.

-Auntie

Postmarked Glen Arbor, date not legible
Mailed to Cadillac, Michigan

Tonawathya

Tonawathya.

In 1901 Frank and Anna Gregory of Chicago purchased some farm land on the west shore of Glen Lake and soon started a summer resort they named Tonawathya. Also known as "Gregory's," the summer resort was run by Anna for several decades. Known as a "rustic health haven," the vacation spot had a faithful clientele, mostly from Chicago. The lodge had ten bedrooms on the second floor for guests. Sometime in the 1910s, rental cottages were added to the resort. Meals featured home-cooked food served family-style using fruits and vegetables from the owner's farm. Recreation was focused on the water with swimming, fishing and boating being the main attractions. The resort was so popular that guests returned only by invitation. Tonawathya changed hands in 1947 when Asa and Edna Case took over the operation. In the 1950s, it changed hands again when Albert Wrisley became the new owner and renamed the resort the Old Orchard Inn. The lodge was burned in the 1970s in a controlled fire department exercise.

Postcard message:

Dear Jo Anne-
Here is where I am vacationing in the bosom of my family -
eating much and sleeping much and having the best time. Glen
Lake is a pretty lake.   *-Hugs & kisses, Emily*

Postmarked Empire, 1939
Mailed to Ann Arbor, Mich.

Tonawathya, Glen Lake.

Old Orchard Inn
(formerly Tonawathya)

"Reached over scenic Highway M-22, on the west shore of Glen Lake, (said to be one of the three most beautiful lakes in the world), Old Orchard Inn and its individual cottages look down over the beautiful waters from a setting among the trees. It is a place of peace, relaxation and rest; a place of joyous vacation activities....

Every form of water sports ... a good beach ... sailboats for rent ... competitive races every week ... canoeing ... boating of all kinds.... Here at Old Orchard Inn are two cement tennis courts ... shuffleboard courts ... badminton, softball ... croquet ... horseshoes ... cards ... indoor tennis ... music ... organized games....

Reading ... our lodge library contains over 2,000 books for your reading pleasure ... with plenty of loafing chairs ... fireplace and delightful surroundings.

You can have accommodations in pleasant outside rooms in the main lodge ... or in rooms in the eight comfortable hotel cottages set among the trees and overlooking the water. All rooms have good beds. Cottages have two, three and four rooms; all have screened porches for loafing. All have bathrooms, electricity, hot and cold running water and complete hotel service. Meals for guests are served in the main lodge dining room."

-Old Orchard Inn - Tonawathya - On Glen Lake, Michigan,
circa 1954

OLD ORCHARD INN

Sylvan Inn
(formerly Grady's)

The Sylvan Inn, built in 1885, is an official Michigan Historic Site. It was sold to George Grady who converted it to Grady's Inn after the town's only hotel, the Walker Inn, burned. Grady offered quarters for lumberjacks working in the area. With the decline of lumbering, the hotel began catering to travelers and tourists and the name was changed to the Sylvan Inn. The hotel advertised its beautiful location and modern conveniences, including innerspring mattresses, hot and cold running water and steam heat. A private beach on Lake Michigan was available for bathing. In addition to the inn, a cottage and cabin were available for rent. The "sylvan" setting on M-109, just off M-22 provided rest and quiet, away from the "roar of traffic." The Inn still operates today, remaining true to its original purpose of providing comfortable, relaxing accommodations in natural surroundings.

The Redwood
Overnight Cabins
In Connection

Horse Shoe Court
Croquet, Ping Pong
Grove Wired for Trailers

Kum-An-Dyne

Mrs. Andresen's

●

Delicious Chicken Dinners

Steak   Fish

●

Glen Arbor — Michigan

On M—22

Kum-an-Dyne

The Kum-an-Dyne was located in Glen Arbor on M-22. Operated by Mrs. M. M. Andresen in the 1930s and 1940s, the restaurant was well-known for its "delicious chicken dinners." Patrons could eat on the shady screened-in porch or inside in the private dining room.

Four redwood overnight cabins were available for rent, each equipped with running water, heat and electricity. Mrs. Andresen also offered spaces for trailers in a pine grove and provided water and electricity for their use. A beach on Lake Michigan drew swimmers and sun-bathers. Other diversions included horseshoes, croquet and ping pong.

Groceries

One building in Glen Arbor has seen a lot of hungry customers. George Dago opened a grocery and dry goods store in Glen Arbor around 1910. As in many small towns, the local grocery store had one of the first telephones. The Dago store was succeeded by the J. M. Hilton store about 1921, when gasoline was offered as a sideline. Steffens' Superette followed in 1945 offering frozen foods, beer for take out and other modern amenities. The Superette became Steffens' IGA in 1962. The Steffens name was well known in Glen Arbor for almost 50 years. In 1994 the business was sold to Brad Anderson who renamed the store Anderson's Market. In 2014 he extensively remodeled the building.

J. M. Hilton
GLEN ARBOR
General Store

Fresh and Smoked   Groceries and
Meats   Provisions

Mobilgas and Mobiloil

Steffen's
Superette

GLEN ARBOR, MICHIGAN

MEATS
F-r-o-z-e-n   F-o-o-d-s
GROCERIES
— Beer to take out —
Fresh Vegetables

Art's Tavern

Glen Arbor's "original gathering place" has been located at the corner of Lake Street and M-22 for over 80 years. It had its origins as the Blue Goose Saloon operated by Frank Sheridan. The tavern was renamed Art's when Frank's son, Art Sheridan, took over the business in 1934. The wooden building was a familiar sight in Glen Arbor until an electrical fire burned the building down in 1950. It was rebuilt in a modern brick style and still stands today. Tim Barr bought the tavern in 2000 and sensibly kept the Art's name. Art's unique atmosphere remains a quaint oasis of northern Michigan charm in a world of chain restaurants and bars. Art's two-headed fish and pennants from colleges and universities add to the comfortable surroundings, drawing customers back generation after generation.

Glen Arbor Gift Shop

The Glen Arbor Gift Shop was opened in 1938 by Robert Oleson and Jack Rader. The following year Rader bought out his partner. The original building was removed in 1947 and a new and larger shop was erected on the site. That same year Jack Rader married Mary Foster and together they ran the store as "Rader's" until 1972 when the business was sold.

The Raders sold "a complete line of sundries to fit the needs of the vacationist," including art and camera supplies, gifts and novelty items. Indian baskets, quill boxes, moccasins, turquoise jewelry and other souvenirs made their way home with many tourists. As a one-stop shop, they rented bicycles, sold live bait and offered ice cream, candy and pop. The Raders also published a line of postcards with scenes from the area which they sold in the store. The store was later expanded and became the Totem Shop, which is still a favorite tourist stop today.

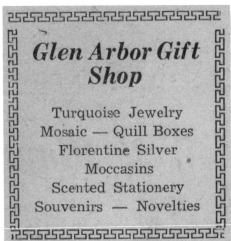

Glen Arbor Gift Shop

Turquoise Jewelry
Mosaic — Quill Boxes
Florentine Silver
Moccasins
Scented Stationery
Souvenirs — Novelties

Postcard message:

Hi Everyone - Just finished taking a dip in beautiful Glen Lake, the cleanest lake water I've ever been in! The weather is ideal - the scenery gorgeous. Having a grand trip so far.

-Debra

Postmarked Glen Arbor, 1945
Mailed to Grand Rapids, Mich.

GLEN ARBOR, MICH.   C-2937

Postcard message:

Hi Peoples;
We are in a nice 3 bedroom knotty pine cabin near Glen Lake. Fishing is swell. John got a large bass last night and big blue gills. We could live on fish. Children are wonderful. Tomorrow we are traveling for a day to take in the sights. John Jr. caught two fish and caused quite a panic in the boat. Elaine is OK. We are all happy.
                                        -Dorothy & John

Postmarked Glen Arbor, date not legible
Mailed to Grand Rapids, Mich.

Crystal River Service Station

The Crystal River Service Station had a prominent location on M-22 at the Crystal River and C-675 (Dunn's Farm Road). The station sold Texaco gasoline and assorted sundries to motorists driving the scenic M-22 route.

Postcard message:

July 16 & 17, 1932
Remember the two patriarch maples on the lawn.
Full moon. Letting Louise and Elinor in, after they
had been locked out.
M-22! That road that went everywhere!

Postcard not mailed.

Bathing in Crystal River at Glen Arbor Mich. 222.

Crystal River

The Crystal River is a beautiful meandering stream starting in Fisher Lake and slowly winding its way to the blue waters of Lake Michigan. The direct span between Fisher Lake and the big lake is only about a mile in actual distance, but the Crystal River, with its twists and turns, winds for about six miles before reaching its destination.

In the autumn, the river is a favorite spot for salmon and steelhead trout fishing. The graceful river provides canoeists and kayakers with a beautiful array of plant life and wildlife along its banks. Groves of pine, cedar, tamarack and birch trees as well as swampland border the river's banks. In the spring there's a profusion of wildflowers. Turtles, frogs, beavers and otters can be spotted. Ducks, swans, herons, bald eagles and other birds make the river banks their natural habitat. Deer come down to the water's edge for a drink.

As M-22 heads north out of Glen Arbor through a parade of tall trees, the road parallels the river offering glimpses of its peaceful water. M-22 crosses the Crystal River just north of C-675 (Dunn's Farm Road).

Crystal River Glen Arbor Mich- H6

Glen Arbor Roller Mills
(formerly the Brammer Mill)

The first grist mill located just outside of Glen Arbor on the Crystal River was built in about 1861, and sold five years later to Thomas Kelderhouse, who tore it down in 1879 and constructed a new mill. Frank Brammer purchased the mill in 1898, and later took out the grinding stones, replacing them with roller mills. Frank operated the mill until his death in 1923. His son August then ran the mill until the 1940s when the dam was blown. The property changed hands several times and was used as a recording studio in the 1970s. The property was purchased in 1986 by Bob Kuras of the Homestead. The Glen Arbor Roller Mills was designated a Michigan Historic Site in 1977.

The Mill, Glen Arbor, Mich.

Camp Leelanau for Boys

William "Skipper" and Cora Beals, both teachers at the Principia College in St. Louis, purchased land in 1923 near the mouth of the Crystal River on Sleeping Bear Bay with the intention of opening a camp for boys from Christian Science families. They had previously leased a summer camp for boys near Grand Haven, but wanted a permanent home for the campers. A roster of 26 boys opened the first season in 1924.

Balanced Summer Program

"Glen Arbor, Michigan.... Boys 6-18. Balanced summer program includes swimming, water skiing, canoeing, camping, trips (by canoe, horseback or hiking), arts and crafts, Indian and Nature lore, competitive sports. The leadership and activities to develop and challenge the abilities and interest of every boy. Known throughout the U.S.A. for its camping philosophy and program.
Arthur S. Huey, President
Thomas Hilton, Camp Director"

-Vacation Days in Michigan's Grand Traverse Bay Region, 1959

Porch at Kohahna

Camp Kohahna

Maude Beals Turner, the younger sister of Skipper Beals, had been encouraged to organize a girls camp for the sisters of the boys at Camp Leelanau. Camp Kohahna for Girls followed closely in the footsteps of Camp Leelanau for Boys and opened as a sister camp in 1924, the same year the boys camp was moved from Grand Haven to the shores of Sleeping Bear Bay. The girls camp was located near Pyramid Point, out of walking range to the boys camp. Maude Beals Turner successfully operated the camp for forty years.

Postcard message:

Sun. noon - Attended the horse show yesterday. Marcia didn't win a prize but she rides very well. She says that she and Wendy are the best tennis players in the squad. I don't know just what that means but will find out today at the tournament. She is also in archery today even tho she had had only one lesson.

-H.R.E.

Postmarked Traverse City, date not legible
Mailed to Detroit Mich.

INTERIOR OF GREAT HOUSE   CAMP KOHAHNA   4

Co-education Thrives

With the success of their two camps, Skipper and Cora Beals, went on to found a school, Leelanau for Boys, in 1929. The first class of fifteen boys lived in summer quarters until the Homestead Lodge was completed that fall. The school grew to become a four-year high school and was accredited in 1933. Requests for a similar school for girls prompted the Beals to open Pinebrook for Girls in 1940 with an enrollment of eight girls. With Skipper's death in 1942, the operation of the schools continued under Arthur "Major" Huey, who had been associated with the the camps since 1929, and his wife, Helen, who was a sister of Cora Beals. They purchased the schools and under their direction, the schools flourished.

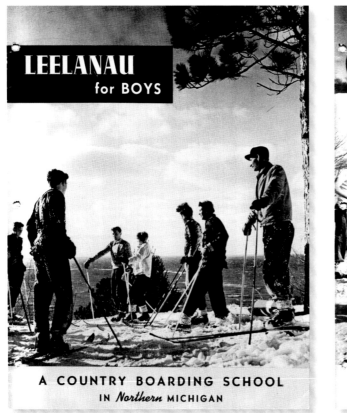 

Leelanau and Pinebrook

"The Leelanau Schools - Pinebrook for Girls and Leelanau for Boys - take their name from the region in which they are located, Leelanau County, one of the most beautiful sections of Michigan's famed north woods. Leelanau, pronounced Lee-la-naw, is an Indian word signifying 'Land of Delight.' The 700 acres of school property lie at the mouth of the Crystal River, a trout stream, which empties into Sleeping Bear Bay of Lake Michigan. The campus has been landscaped to provide restful lawns and clear vistas without disturbing the natural beauty of the woods. Glen Arbor, the school post office, is about 340 miles from Chicago and 280 miles from Detroit.... Good roads reach Leelanau County from all points."

-Pinebrook for Girls: A Country Boarding School, circa 1950

Boarding School Life

The boys boarding at Leelanau for Boys spent the school year in a beautiful spot in the north woods of Leelanau County. Each student had his own desk, dresser, closet and bed. The rooms were paneled in knotty pine and windows revealed scenic views. The boys were required to make their own beds, and keep their living quarters clean. Besides the sound scholastic training, they enjoyed a vigorous outdoor and athletic program, including skiing, football, basketball, tennis, horseback riding, golf and track. Boys were given the chance to earn money at an hourly rate and gain valuable work experience by doing gardening, landscaping and maintenance work. The school uniform consisted of a camel's hair jacket, white shirt, brown slacks and tie. The uniform was worn for dinner, Sunday School, and social events.

Academic Life

Students at the Leelanau Schools studied U.S. history, algebra, geometry, biology, botany, Latin, and other traditional high school subjects. Classes were small and some were coeducational. Individual instruction was available in art, music and speech. Leelanau for Boys prepared its male students for a life of "cultured refinement," poise and inner strength, and the "satisfying experience of learning how to work and to earn." Pinebrook for Girls readied its female students with the skills needed to be "happy, successful homemakers," but also prepared them for college and a career outside the home if a girl wanted to pursue that direction.

Beginning of the Homestead

The Leelanau Homestead had its start in a lodge built for Leelanau for Boys. Parents needed a place to stay when visiting their children, so starting in 1930, guest rooms at the Homestead were used. As the number of camp and school buildings grew, so did available options for summer rental. Riveredge, shown below, was a dormitory for the Pinebrook girls, but used by the Homestead as one of the guest buildings during the summer months. Promotional materials advertised the "modern conveniences such as heat and private baths with the graciousness of home living." Services included daily maid services, meals, and use of the library.

Major and Helen Huey fixed up a few rustic cabins and charged $5 a night to visiting parents and summer guests. These early overnight rentals laid the groundwork for the future resort. By the 1950s these pine-paneled cabins featured beds so comfortable that you could "sleep like a bear."

The Leelanau Schools

Three entities fell under the Leelanau Schools umbrella: Camp Leelanau for Boys; Pinebrook for Girls and Leelanau for Boys; and The Homestead, all on 1,200 acres of beautiful northern Michigan property. When Major and Helen Huey retired in the 1960s, this organization was dissolved. The Leelanau School was incorporated as a non-profit and the camp was operated as a limited partnership. The Homestead was sold and slowly grew from a few buildings and cottages used as summer vacation rentals when school was not in session, into the prestigious resort that it is today.

The Leelanau Homestead

"The Leelanau Homestead ... one of America's outstanding family resorts, in scenic surroundings, where the north woods meet the turquoise blue of Sleeping Bear Bay.

The inn, modern guest cottages, play area, white sand beaches, woodland trails, trout streams, on more than 300 acres of grounds - 'like a country estate of your own.'

Pack and head for vacation 'as you like it.' Fun and games or peace and quiet ... that's the way at the Leelanau Homestead. Swim, play tennis or shuffleboard, ride horseback, take part in planned social activities if you wish. Or, feel free to rest undisturbed or explore 'on your own' the byways around Sleeping Bear Bay.

Guests rave about our delicious, home-cooked meals skillfully served in the new 'picture window' terrace dining room overlooking Lake Michigan.... Children are welcome at the Homestead. Sitters are available for those times when parents might choose to go on a 'jaunt' of their own.

Beach picnics, 'float' trips down the Platte River, climbing the incomparable Sleeping Bear Sand Dunes, trips to nearby points of interest - all these are included in summer fun at the Homestead."

-*The Leelanau Homestead*, circa 1957

HAVE A COLORFUL VACATION IN THE LAND OF THE SLEEPING BEAR DUNES

Towering deep-green pines meet wide, white sandy beaches along deep-blue Lake Michigan . . . at The Homestead. You command 400 acres of private grounds . . . hills, woods, streams, shoreline . . . offering every recreation or quiet solitude. Luxurious rooms are beautifully furnished, with family cottages available. Dine, American Plan, and enjoy superb foods . . . with beach suppers and special buffets often featured. Special summer courses are offered in the arts, and a World Affairs Symposium brings distinguished world editors and personages to The Homestead to speak on vital topics of interest. Write for free color-brochure and information.

LEELANAU'S FAMOUS GUEST INN...ON THE
SLEEPING BEAR BAY OF LAKE MICHIGAN

The Homestead

ARTHUR S. HUEY, PRES.   •   GLEN ARBOR, MICHIGAN   •   PHONE: EDISON 4-3041

VISITORS DINE WITH US AT THE HOMESTEAD • USE THE LEELANAU LIBRARY ON THE GROUNDS

Manitou View

Bids You Welcome

FRED J. MILLER, Proprietor

Post Office, Maple City, R 3
Phone, Port Oneida Ex.

Sunday Dinners
by Appointment

Lake Frontage for
Beautiful Home Sites

Manitou View Inn

The Manitou View Inn was located about two miles north of Glen Arbor, just off M-22 on Thoreson Road. The Inn was so named because of its view of the Manitou Islands from the high bluff on which the inn was built. The Inn was operated by Fred and Ellen Miller in the 1920s. Guests stayed in the bedrooms upstairs and meals were served family-style in the dining room. Meals were prepared by Ellen Miller, who was an excellent cook. Chicken, steak and fish dinners were also available by appointment for guests not staying at the Inn. Arrangements for taxi service were made with nearby resorts to bring hungry dinner guests to the Manitou View Inn. Parents and guests of Camp Leelanau for Boys were referred to the Manitou View Inn before accommodations were built on the Homestead property. Unfortunately, the Inn burned in 1930, and all that remains is the fieldstone arch leading to the property.

SEE GLEN MAGIC

MYSTIFYING FORCES OF GRAVITY

Entertainment for the Entire Family

- **Free Picnic Area**
- **Swings and Slides for the Kiddies**
- **Guided Tours**

On M-22, 7 miles north of Glen Arbor

June 15 to September 9   Hours: Daily — 10 A. M. to 10 P. M.

Glen Magic

The 1960s were a time of magic and mystery if one were to believe that such places as the Mystery Spot in St. Ignace, Mystery Hill in the Irish Hills and Mystery Ridge located between East Tawas and Oscoda, could really stop the forces of gravity. Leelanau County had its own "mystery spot" in the crooked house of Glen Magic, located on M-22, about seven miles north of Glen Arbor. Here the "mystifying forces of gravity" were suspended for the whole family's entertainment. Picnic tables and a playground for the children rounded out the fun.

Postcard message:

August 15, 1957
Visited this place with our church group from St.
Francis. Very interesting art. Nice picnic lunch,
sunny day.

Postcard not mailed.

Lund's Scenic Garden

"The Garden is 22 miles from Traverse City, by way of Cedar and Maple City, 40 miles from Frankfort, 35 miles from Beulah and 9 miles north of Glen Lake on M-22....

We believe that the garden is the only one of its kind in existence. Each of the scenes portray an important event taken from the life of our Lord while he walked the shores of Galilee....

The garden was dedicated on August 15, 1948, and is considered the most beautiful religious spot in northern Michigan."

-Lund's Scenic Garden, circa 1950

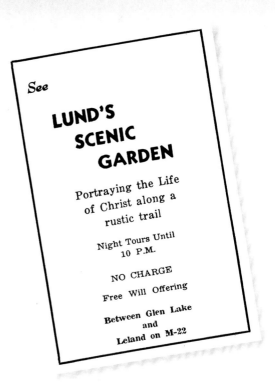

Most Unusual Attraction

Rev. Earl Kline Lund and his wife, Rev. Orpha Lund, both ordained ministers in the United Brethren Church, created a most unusual tourist attraction. The self-trained artists painted life-size cutouts and scenes depicting the life of Christ, his death and resurrection, then placed them along a 1,400-foot sawdust-covered trail in a cedar swamp forest. The Lunds opened the Garden in 1948, and by the time it closed in 1987, they had created a total of 30 scenes and some 300 cutout figures

The religious attraction was visited by as many as 10,000 visitors in a summer season. People from all over the United States, Canada, China and other countries came in droves. Many church groups, Sunday School classes, and various clubs toured the Garden. Rev. E.K. Lund recorded an L.P. record featuring "The Story and Recorded Tour of Lund's Scenic Gardens." The roadside attraction received much publicity and a fair amount of recognition from folk art critics. Jane and Michael Stern in their book, *Amazing America*, compared the artwork to a "Rousseau painting, but with a religious theme" and said that viewing the staged sets was like looking into "an ornate Easter egg."

161

Traverse Lake Resort
(formerly Atkinson's)

The Traverse Lake Resort was located on M-22 midway between Glen Arbor and Leland on the shore of Traverse Lake. The Atkinson family established the resort about 1904 with the name Traverse Lake Resort, but it was widely known as Atkinson's. The resort changed hands in 1937 when George and Cora Kelderhouse purchased the resort and renovated it. The large white tourist home advertised soft beds, in cool, clean well-lighted rooms. The inn offered excellent dining room service with family-style meals and Sunday chicken dinners. An early advertisement warned "You'll likely gain weight here." Besides the reputation for excellent food, the resort was well-known among fishermen for successful catches of bass, perch and pickerel in the waters of Traverse Lake. In later years the inn changed hands several times while continuing the tradition of fine dining and accommodations in this landmark building.

TRAVERSE LAKE RESORT
ON M-22
MAPLE CITY - MICH.

Postcard message:

Aug. 29
Arrived safely at 6:30 Found good beds in a tourist home. Had a real fish supper! Roads very good but rain all the way from Cadillac. Fishing at Traverse Lake tomorrow morning - it should be good.

-Best wishes, Hank

Postmarked Maple City, 1939
Mailed to Lowell, Mich.

"Atkinsons" Traverse Lake, Maple City, Mich.

Postcard message:

Dear Folks;-
The weather here has been wonderful. Everything is
pretty - the roadsides are lined with forget-me-nots and wild columbine.
We've seen so much white trillium!

-Love, Charlie & Edith

Postmarked Cedar, 1952
Mailed to Cadillac, Mich.

Shetland School

No longer used as a school, the little red schoolhouse still stands proudly along M-22 in Cleveland Township. The old Shetland School was built about 1871. The building was restored and remodeled in 1973 by Mary Lou and Tom Blakely for their antique store, the School Bell and Apple. It is now a private residence. The old red schoolhouse is a popular stop for photographic shoots and has been used in advertising pieces over the years.

Good Harbor Trout Preserve

The Good Harbor Trout Preserve on M-22, was situated on a spring-fed stream in a natural wooded area. It was located five miles south of Leland. As a private establishment there was no limit to the number of fish caught and no license required. Claims were made that a catch of trout up to 30 inches was not unusual. The Preserve also sold fresh rainbow trout "netted while you watch us." An advertisement from 1957 proclaims "Big, Plump Fish, making four generous servings - cleaned, ready for the pan for 97 cents." The business was open all year and customers could order fish for winter shipment.

Lime Lake from Sugar Loaf, Maple City, Mich.

Trail to Sugar Loaf Mountain, Mich.

Traverse Lake from Sugar Loaf

Sugar Loaf Mountain

Before Sugar Loaf Mountain became a winter skiing center, it was known as one of the best viewing spots in Leelanau County. A path was created for an easy, but long, hike to the top. It made for a nice day's excursion with a picnic lunch and a pleasant rest at the summit. Sugar Loaf Mountain's elevation is about 800 feet, and from that height views of Lime Lake, Traverse Lake, Bass Lake, Shell Lake and Lake Michigan could be seen. On a clear day, North and South Manitou Islands could be spotted rising up from Lake Michigan. Sugar Loaf is named for the fact that it appears to be shaped like an old-fashioned loaf of sugar, particularly when it is glistening with snow.

Part of the Sugar Loaf property was owned by the county. A committee of Leelanau citizens with the cooperation of the local American Legion post, convinced the county to purchase an additional 400 acres in 1940 for a potential winter sports park. Nothing developed during WWII, but in 1945 the Sugar Loaf Winter Sports Club was established with Major Huey of the Leelanau Schools as its president. Peppi Teichner was hired in 1946 as the club manager and the new facility opened to the public on January 1, 1947.

Winter Sports at Sugar Loaf Mt. South of Leland, Mich.

Sugar Loaf MOUNTAIN WINTER SPORTS CENTER of Leelanau County

Opening Day

"With twenty inches of excellent skiing snow, Sugar Loaf, the middle west's newest winter sports park, nine miles south of Leland in Leelanau County, formally opened New Year's Day.

Peppi Teichner, ski professional and instructor, said the snow was the best he had seen for fast skiing and announced that the ski tow, the first in Northwestern Michigan, worked satisfactorily. The warming house was opened and hot lunches were served to the opening day crowd.

The park will not be formally dedicated until February 23 when the Central Ski Association down-hill run and slalom contests will be held there. All skiers who wish to qualify for the Olympic games in the central division must participate in this contest.

A parking lot has been provided for the winter sports fans near the ski runs. A small parking charge and a small admission fee to the grounds are charged. Ski tow is $1.50 for a half day or $2.50 for all day.

Weather permitting, the ski runs will be operated straight through until Spring."

-*Northport Tribune*, January 2, 1947

Fine Winter Sports Area

"A three-quarter-mile-long main ski slope, an outstanding slalom bowl and excellent facilities for learning to ski have combined to make Sugar Loaf Mountain of Michigan's famous Leelanau peninsula one of the state's fine winter sports areas.

Under the supervision of of Hans 'Peppi' Teichner, internationally known professional skier, hundreds of students at nearby Leelanau Schools have learned to ski at Sugar Loaf.

The main slope at Sugar Loaf starts from an elevation of 700 feet. This run and others in the area are served by four tow ropes. A slow-running tow serves the beginners area. The slalom bowl at Sugar Loaf is popular with ski racers who come here to train.

Sugar Loaf Mountain is ideally designed for downhill, slalom or cross-country skiing, and from the peak of the slopes are rare views of the scenic country that has brought fame to Leelanau County.

Sugar Loaf is situated midway between Leland and Glen Arbor on M-22 and is 17 miles northwest of Traverse City. The area is open to the public every Sunday. Fees for use of all facilities, including the shelter house, are $1 daily for adults and 35 cents for students."

-Winter Sports in West Michigan, 1954

Sugar Loaf had a small airstrip so that skiers with private planes could fly up north for a quick weekend of winter sport.

For Advanced or Novice Skiiers

SUGARLOAF Mountain

on the Leelanau Peninsula

Four rope tows to serve East and West slopes and a magnificent slalom bowl.

Expert instruction by Hans (Peppi) Teichner of Sun Valley and Aspen fame.

Situated on M-22, between Glen Arbor and Leland.

Housing and eating conveniently close.

All Skiing and shelter house facilities available at a daily fee of $1 for adults, 35 cents for students.

Open to public every Sunday during season from 1:00 to 5:00.

For Information Write

H. H. TEICHNER
R. F. D. No. 1, CEDAR, MICHIGAN

Leelanau Ski School

"Sugar Loaf Mountain - a new winter sports area offering skiing facilities of all varieties - for beginners, intermediates, and advanced - ski tows, warming house, instruction, magnificent scenery at the summit - Leelanau students are organized in classes from beginners to experts and receive professional instruction in the Leelanau Ski School - other winter sports such as skating and ice hockey are included in the program."

-Leelanau in Color, 1950

Jolli-Lodge

The Jolli-Lodge has been accommodating Leelanau County visitors for over 50 years. The lodge is located on M-22 on the shore of Lake Michigan about three miles south of Leland and five miles north of Sugar Loaf. The resort was opened in 1956 by the Jolliffe family and is still in family hands. The resort has rooms in the lodge and also cottages and apartments available for rent. In the early days, dinners and luncheons were available to the public by reservation. When Sugar Loaf Mountain was in its glory days in the 1960s, the resort was open year round. The home-like atmosphere of the resort has welcomed generation after generation of families who come back for the weekly potlucks, marshmallow roasts and dazzling sunsets.

Lake View Farm Resort

Some farmers opened their homes to visitors when the tourist industry in Leelanau was burgeoning. A farm vacation was promoted as a wholesome escape from hectic city life. Lake View Farm, located about three miles south of Leland, had accommodations for 25 guests. It advertised that it provided all the modern conveniences, such as hot and cold water, gaslight, large airy rooms, telephone, and mail delivery daily. A large lawn with plenty of shade surrounded the main building. The resort also offered "fine tenting grounds" on the shore of Lake Michigan. The century-old lodge on M-22 continues the tradition of welcoming guests as the Snowbird Inn Bed and Breakfast.

M-22 near Leland

Motorists driving along M-22 near
Leland have frequent views of the
beautiful blue waters of North Lake
Leelanau. Never far from the water,
the winding road passes along lovely
woodlands and handsome cottages
before entering the charming village
where M-22 crosses the Leland River.

Leland, Mich.

Leland, Mich.

Postcard message:

Hello Kiddos,
We are on our vacation, having a very pleasant
time in Michigan. Lots of beautiful drives here.
Wonderful weather. Plenty of fish dinners, etc.
Never saw such pretty lakes.

Bud and Marge

Postmarked Leland, 1945
Mailed to Chicago, Ill.

Van's Garage

Van's Garage

EXPERT

MECHANICAL SERVICE

LUBRICATION SERVICE

CAR WASHING

Phone—Lake Leelanau 22F21

Van's Garage has been a mainstay in Leland for over 80 years. The current location at 112 South Main Street, was built in 1929 by Carroll Stander as an automobile garage and Graham Paige dealership. The following year, John K. Van Raalte from Holland, Michigan headed north in search of work as an auto mechanic and landed a job with Stander. The Great Depression hit the automotive business hard and Stander had to let his employees go in 1933, but continued to operate until 1935 when he was forced to close the business. The State of Michigan bought the building and used it as a State Highway Garage until the beginning of World War II.

Finding himself without work and not wanting to leave his adopted home of Leland, John Van Raalte decided to team up with his brother Albert and opened the first Van's Garage - a Texaco gas station on Main Street, south of the river. John left for WWII and when he returned to Leland he and Albert bought the current building at 112 Main Street and sold Mobil gasoline, tires and auto parts, and offered auto repair. The careful work that Van's does on antique and collectible cars seems an appropriate use for this historical building.

Postcard message:

Dear Grandma,
Arrived here safe and sound. It is a lovely place here and I
know we will enjoy it. This is a bridge that we cross to go to
our cottage. We have a view of the lake.
                              -With love, Mary Jane

p.s. We enjoyed the cake ever so much.

Postmarked Leland, 1919
Mailed to Fort Wayne, Indiana

Leland Bridge

The postcard above shows the iron bridge crossing the Leland River (Carp River). This bridge was built about 1906, replacing an older smaller bridge built on cedar pilings. The new concrete bridge shown on the left, was completed in 1929. A temporary bridge was built so traffic could continue while the new concrete bridge was being constructed.

Leland, Mich.

Fishtown

The Leland River (Carp River), emptying into Lake Michigan at Leland, was once known as the "place where the Indians run their canoes up the river." As early as 1880 commercial fishermen began to use the river as their home port. Small sailboats were used by the fishermen until gas-powered boats came on the scene about 1900. A harbor was developed to provide an entrance for the fishing boats. By 1920 eight fishing crews operated out of "Fishtown." They caught whitefish and trout by the ton. Fishing peaked about 1930 and then declined because of overfishing, the introduction of invasive species, and regulations favoring sport fishing.

Wooden fishing shanties, over-hanging docks, icehouses and smokehouses were built during the first three decades of the twentieth century. The quaint charm of this working fishing village drew tourists as early as the 1920s. Now the remaining weather-beaten buildings lining the river boardwalk house one remaining fishery, gift shops and other attractions that still draw in thousands of tourists each summer.

Fishtown was designated as a Michigan Historic Site in 1973 and was placed on the National Register of Historic Places in 1975. It received a Michigan Historical marker in 1977 from the Michigan Historical Commission. Fishtown is currently owned and managed by the Fishtown Preservation Society.

Fishing Fleet in Harbor Leland Mich N7

Postcard Message:

Dear Minnie,
Does this not look restful to you? Does it not have
more appeal than the seething maelstrom of Detroit?
We are having a wonderful time. Fishing - few
catches, watching fishermen here - big catches.
                              -Love, Harry

Postmarked Leland, 1939
Mailed to Detroit, Mich.

Postcard message:

We had a delightful drive of 160 miles last Sunday
through Leland, Northport, and Traverse City. These
fishing barges at Leland took Bud's fancy. He would
have stayed all day prowling around them. The kiddies
had a wonderful time in the waves. Altho it has been
cool, they have been in almost every day. We expect to
leave for home two weeks from today and hope to drive
through in one day.

                              -Love, G.R.W.

Postmarked Leland, 1927
Mailed to Terre Haute, Ind.

Leland, Mich.

Fascinating Nets

Large nets were used by fishermen to catch whitefish, chubs and lake trout. The cotton nets were reeled onto outdoor drying racks which kept them from rotting and made it easier for resetting on the next journey out. Holes were easier to spot on the racks and more manageable to repair. The fishermen used special cotton twine and "fisherman's knots" in a craft similar to crocheting to fix the tears caused by thrashing fish or debris caught in the nets. Tourists were fascinated, watching the complicated maneuvers of mending the nets. George Cook, shown here at the left, always had a pipe in his mouth, and with his white hair and jaunty cap, was a colorful model for photographers and artists. The Leland fisherman played the part well of an "old salt" in his later years.

On the Horizon

The shores of the Leland Harbor offered a great spot for boat watching. Besides the commercial fishing boats operating out of Fishtown, visitors as well as locals, enjoyed watching for the mail boat coming back from the Manitou Islands, the occasional Coast Guard ship out on the lake, and the nautical color provided by private yachts and launches. Sunset watching was then, as it is now, a popular ritual for all ages.

For those who wanted a view from the water, Erhardt Peters offered scenic boat rides on Lake Michigan to Good Harbor Bay, Pyramid Point, the Manitou Islands and other interesting spots in the area. These sight-seeing trips offered opportunities for the fisherman to troll for trout, for the camera bug to catch on film the scenic beauty of the dunes from the water, and others to simply enjoy an outing on the fresh water of Lake Michigan.

The *Lawrence*

The *Lawrence* was the first boat to provide both mail and passenger service to the Manitou Islands. The gas-powered launch operated out of the Leland harbor at Fishtown. John Paetschow piloted the vessel from 1904 until approximately 1920, when Paetschow's brother-in-law, Tracey Grovesner who had been apprenticing, took over.

Leland

It's hard to imagine now that the charming village of Leland was once the site of a grimy, smoky iron furnace in the 1870s. For 14 years, between 1870 and 1884, Leland was a boom town thanks to the success of the Leland Lake Superior Iron Company. In 1883 the company even promised to build a courthouse, so the county seat was moved from Northport to Leland. The boom came to an end the following year when the company ceased operation. Shortly thereafter the Leland Lumber Company was formed, a sawmill was built, and for the next 15 years the main industry in the Leland area was lumbering. When lumbering died out about 1900, the future of Leland looked bleak. But soon vacationers ventured north, lured by the beauty of the region and the temperate climate. Leland's location on a strip of land between Lake Michigan and Lake Leelanau was a natural point for the growth of the tourist industry. Hotels and cottages were built and the summer population swelled. As more and more vacationers arrived by automobile, services such as gas stations, garages, stores and restaurants followed. M-22, the Main Street of Leland, saw an increase in automobile traffic both from those making Leland their destination and those passing through.

Leland Mercantile Co.

"Everything from a Needle to a Steamship"

General Merchandise

Leland, Michigan

Leland Mercantile

The Leland Mercantile has been a fixture in Leland for over 100 years. The general store, operated by the Cordes brothers, was first located in the Harbor House building, but moved across River Street when the business was incorporated in 1906. The store was a hub of activity and had one of the few telephones in town in the early part of the 20th century. The Mercantile carried a wide array of merchandise to serve its diverse patrons, which included everyone from local fishermen to wealthy summer resorters. Besides groceries, the store featured dry goods, clothing and shoes, sporting goods, Indian baskets, camera supplies, hardware items and other articles. In the 1930s the Mercantile had a gas pump out front and sold Shell gasoline. To highlight this variety of goods, the store once used the slogan, "everything from a Needle to a Steamship" - a bit of hyperbole. The store had an ice cream parlor, a butcher shop and sold blocks of ice for the home ice-box. The hardware section was located in the basement. In 1953 the business became a Spartan Store, and the building was modernized in the 1960s. Throughout the years the store has remained a vital part of the community.

EMIL PEDERSEN
General Merchandise
S. D. D. Liquor - Wine - Beer
Fishing Tackle and Licenses
LELAND

Prosperous Business Community

"Leland is a prosperous, picturesque settlement" said the *Traverse City Record Eagle* on July 31, 1926, "boasting stores … where all of the creature wants of summer guests can be cared for." There were hotels, tourist homes and cottages to accommodate visitors. Stores in Leland did more than cater to summer visitors. They served the local population as well with two general stores, a barber shop, two auto garages, two boat liveries and two restaurants. Emil Pedersen ran a general store, but was also a baker, confectioner, insurance salesman and real estate agent- certainly a man of all trades.

New Hotel Leelanau

The New Hotel Leelanau, also known as the Anderson Hotel, was built about 1900 on the northeastern corner of River and Main Streets. A 1912 tourist brochure from the Manistee & Northeastern Railroad stated, "Under the efficient management of Mr. H.S. Anderson, this commercial hotel has its share of summer visitors, and pays especial heed to the wants and comforts of fishermen." The hotel burned down about 1920 and was not rebuilt.

Post Office, Leland, Mich.

Leland Post Office

As in many small towns, the Leland Post Office changed locations over the years. The first post office may have been located in the home of Antoine Manseau, the first white man to put down roots in Leland in 1852. After a couple of other sites, the post office shown in this postcard, postmarked 1936, was located on the east side of Main Street, which later housed a succession of women's clothing stores. In the 1950s the post office was located on the west side of the street, next door to the Harbor House building. The post office at its current location opened to the public in December 1961.

The Blue Bird

The Blue Bird started out in 1927 as a simple sandwich and soda shop serving short orders, home-baked bread, pies, cakes and ice cream. Sidelines included candy, cigarettes, soft drinks and Indian baskets. Martin and Leone Telgard were the proprietors.

The business slowly developed into a full-service restaurant in the following years, eventually expanding to the present 10,000 square feet. In the 1940s and 1950s the Bluebird (now spelled as one word) was the place to go for dinner and dancing. Bands such as the Five Shades of Blue, Fred Gleason and His Music, and the Champagne Brothers were featured. Advertisements from this period proclaimed, "You'll have a good time if you dance at the Bluebird." Specialties of the restaurant were fried lake trout and whitefish, homemade pies and cinnamon rolls.

The Bluebird occasionally hosted special events. One such event was sponsored by the Leland Sportsman's Club in 1953 with the invitation to "Put on your red shirt and come to the venison supper at the Blue Bird Dining Room." The restaurant is still in the Telgard family and is a favorite gathering spot where many anniversaries, birthdays and other special events are celebrated.

THE RIVERSIDE INN
SCHWARZ SISTERS
ROOMS WITH PRIVATE BATHS
COTTAGES IN CONNECTION

Home Cooking, Home Made Ice Cream, Butter, Eggs, Milk
and Cream fresh from the farm daily.

Eat and Sleep at the Waters' Edge

LELAND   MICHIGAN

Riverside Inn

The original Riverside Inn, built in 1901 by Jacob Schwarz, was located across the street from its current location. In 1912 Schwarz built a boathouse near the Inn on the Leland River (Carp River). The following year the building was converted into a dance hall. Schwarz operated the Inn until his death in 1917. When his wife died the following year, the business was passed on to the couple's daughters, Blanche and Anna. They ran the Inn in the original location until it burned in 1924. Rather than build an entirely new structure, the sisters remodeled the dance hall and moved it parallel to the river. The building was reworked to function as an inn and a second story was added with nine bedrooms. The new Riverside Inn opened in 1925 at its current location. Blanche Schwarz operated the Inn until 1957. The Inn had a fine reputation for its home-cooked meals and served fish dinners daily. The Schwarz brothers operated a boat livery in connection with the Inn and rented boats for fishing expeditions. New owners over the years have enlarged and renovated the Inn and expanded the dining facilities. The Riverside Inn, still a landmark in Leland today, is listed on the National Register of Historic Places.

The New Nicholas Hotel, Leland, Mich.

New Nicholas

The original Nicholas Hotel was built in 1909, but burned in 1926. Frank Rosman, owner of the Hotel, quickly rebuilt in its place a new structure costing $45,000. The New Nicolas Hotel opened in June of 1927. It was built on a small bluff slightly back from Lake Leelanau, with a wonderful view of the lake. The Hotel had its own private bathing beach. The golf course of the Leland Country Club abutted the property, with views of the greens seen from the New Nicolas' verandah. The dining room, 50 feet by 65 feet, was built to seat nearly 500 people with views either toward the lake or toward the village. Plans to use the dining room in the summer for dances were figured into the layout. Rachel's Tea Room operated in connection with the Hotel and offered a la carte service. The large lobby, 18 feet by 50 feet, had a massive fireplace to warm guests on cool evenings. The Hotel was outfitted throughout with new wicker furniture. The bedrooms were unusually large for a hotel. Each room had electric lights and a bathroom with hot and cold running water. Ice water from the hotel's own refrigeration system was a modern amenity at the time. Western Union Telegraph service was available in the office. The New Nicolas Hotel also had cottages available for rent. In 1946 the Hotel became the Leland Lodge, which is still operating in the same location today.

Cottages at The New Nicholas Hotel, Leland, Mich.

Leland Lodge, Leland Mich.

Leland Lodge
(formerly the New Nicholas)

"...Our reputation for excellent food and pleasant living is enviable, and the discriminating will realize that it is no happenstance. Constant care and thoughtful effort are devoted to providing the finest available in food, its preparation, and its service. Our staff of college student waitresses add much to the cheerful dining room, and the musically inclined have been known to provide impromptu bits of song! Our accommodations are simple but completely modern and adequate ... and the cottages have the added cheer of a fireplace for crisp evenings. The long comfortable screened porches of the Lodge catch inviting breezes on warm days.... Any room you choose has its own bath, and the double rooms are spacious with twin beds. The cottages are not equipped for housekeeping, but complete hotel service is provided from the Lodge. All accommodations are American Plan only, and reservations are advisable.... You'll find us up on Michigan's little finger, the lovely Leelanau County.... located on Scenic Highway M-22, a delightful drive that travels the edge of Lake Michigan."

-Leland Lodge - Your Summer Way of Life, circa 1950

Fine Summer Homes

"Leland, at the foot of Lake Leelanau, is one of the most rapidly growing resort colonies of the whole Grand Traverse Summer Land. Here Lake Leelanau empties into Lake Michigan. The pine-clad bluffs between the greater and lesser lakes have been eagerly seized as beautiful cottage sites by delighted vacationists who return season after season to enjoy the great lake breezes, the bathing, rowing, fishing and sailing. Fine summer homes dot the wooded shores."

-*Grand Traverse the Summer Land,* circa 1915

Leland Yacht Club

The Leland Yacht Club, located on North Lake Leelanau in the village of Leland was incorporated in 1936. The following years saw a lot of activity. A pier in Nedow's Bay was built, the area for a swimming beach was cleared, and funds were secured for a qualified lifeguard and swimming instructor. The Club has served as the focal point for water sports on Lake Leelanau for generations. Of course, the favorite and most extensive activity of the Club was sailing. Regular sailing regattas were sponsored by the Club throughout the summer to the delight of sailors and spectators alike. The private Club still sponsors an annual boat parade in August.

Leland Country Club

The Leland Country Club was originally called the Leland Golf Club when it was founded in 1914 by a group of Leland cottage owners. The club had a nine-hole course for golf, which later was enlarged to eighteen holes, and tennis courts. A new clubhouse with a large screened-in porch overlooking Lake Leelanau was built in 1927, but moved about ten years later for a "more sightly view." Clubhouse privileges were extended to members of the Leland Yacht Club in a reciprocal agreement for the use of its dock and swimming beach on Nedow's Bay. In the 1930s "social memberships" for dances were sold to visitors and hotel guests, with the "usual exchange of guest cards" between the Leland Country Club and the Northport Point Country Club. In 1952 the Leland Country Club formally purchased the assets of the Leland Golf Club, and remains a private club today.

THE CLUB HOUSE AT THE COUNTRY CLUB   LELAND, MICH.   F971

Mrs. Maro

Announces the
BLUE LANTERN
at
Leland on M 22
is open for the season, and is serving
Luncheons and Dinners by appointment, With "Alonzo" in charge
of the dinning room

Afternoon Tea

*Blue Lantern Tea Room,
Leland. Mich.*

Blue Lantern Tea Room

The Blue Lantern Tea Room, established in 1923 by Mrs. Maro, was located about one mile north of Leland on the shore of Lake Leelanau. It soon gained a fine reputation as the place to go for luncheons and afternoon tea. Dinner and bridge parties were also available by appointment. The tea room was brightly decorated with painted furniture and colorful wall hangings. Meals were served in the tea house, on the porch, or under sun umbrellas on the lawn. Mrs. Maro raised all her own vegetables and the food served was always fresh and delicious. Mrs. Maro was the widow of "The Great Maro, Prince of Magic." One of his apprentices was Alzono, who came north for the summers to serve as Mrs. Maro's waiter and was one of the leading reasons for the popularity of the tea room. In the early years, the tea room offered a "select line" of oriental novelties and color prints. Handmade children's dresses and ladies lingerie were also for sale in the adjoining cottage. Mrs. Maro also rented furnished cottages and offered lake-front lots for sale adjoining the tea room property.

Happy Hour Tavern

The Happy Hour Tavern was opened in 1936 on M-22 by Joseph Korson. Witban Robert Butler purchased the business in 1948 and continued the business until 1971. Butler brought in an occasional musical act such as Don Widon with his accordion and solovox to liven up the joint. Mr. and Mrs. Stanley Fischer became the next owners and changed the name to Fischer's Happy Hour Tavern. Now a third generation family business, the tavern is owned by Paul Fischer. The watering hole has always been a community gathering spot for locals as well as travelers on the beautiful stretch of scenic M-22 between Leland and Northport.

Happy Hour Tavern

BEER AND WINE

—

BEER AND WINE
TO TAKE OUT

On M-22 between
Northport and Leland

WITBAN BUTLER

Phone EVergreen 6-3881

Northport, Mich.

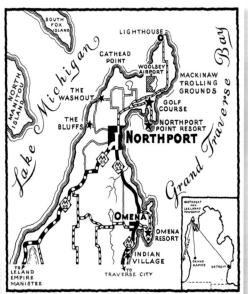

Northport

Northport is situated near the tip of the Leelanau Peninsula, facing the eastern shores of Grand Traverse Bay. The original settlement, Waukazooville, was established in 1849 when Chief Peter Waukazoo and Reverend George Smith moved with 40 or 50 Native American families from Holland, Michigan to the tip of the Leelanau Peninsula. Three years later in 1852, Deacon Joseph Dame platted the present village, named it Northport, and annexed nearby Waukazooville.

Northport was the largest settlement in Leelanau County in the 1850s until the early 1900s. Village life centered on the harbor, an important port of call for schooners and steamers. Lumbering and fishing were the main industries. Cherry cultivation started in 1853 when Reverend George Smith planted his first cherry trees, and the cherry industry continued to play an important economic role in Northport for about 100 years.

Tourism developed as steamships and the railroad brought vacationers to Northport. Hotels, cottages and resorts were built. Automobile traffic increased as roads were improved. M-22 brought motorists to the tip of the peninsula for sightseeing tours and vacation stays. Tourist cottages and a tourist camp catered to the new breed of vacationing motorists. The village of Northport with its historic buildings and waterfront heritage is still a destination point today.

Hotel Northern

C-3274

HOTEL NORTHERN NORTHPORT MICH

The Hotel Northern, located on Waukazoo Street (M-22), was opened in the late 1910s by Ole Fredrickson. The Metevier family owned the business in the early 1920s. By the mid-1920s Bert Ellis had become the proprietor. He enlarged the hotel and established its reputation for fish dinners served every day. The business changed hands in 1929 when the Vannetters bought the hotel and restaurant, and for a while the restaurant was known as the "Spotless Cafe." They added beer and wine next door in the "Silver Room."

The Hotel Northern was a favorite stop for fishermen in the 1940s. The Mackinaw Trout trolling camps brought lots of eager fishermen to Northport. The Hotel Northern offered to cook fish caught by its guests. After WWII the business became known as Shepherd's Dining Room. In the next few decades new owners featured live music and dancing. Woody's Settling Inn operated in the spot from 1978 to 2004. The building was razed and Tucker's of Northport opened on the site in 2014.

Budd Cottage

The Budd Cottage was located on Nagonaba Street, just a block off M-22 as one enters Northport from the south. Mrs. Martha Voice Budd opened the tourist home and restaurant about 1900. Ida Budd took over the business when Mrs. Martha Budd died and operated it until the late 1920s when Mrs. Viola Gagnon bought the property. The Budd Cottage had a trout stream running through the backyard, and large maple trees that provided cool shade for the guests. In 1938 Mrs. Floyd Leonde bought the business and advertised "southern cooking" in a "homelike atmosphere." By 1939 the inn was owned by Blanche and Emery Bence. They later changed the name to "The Village Inn" and operated it as a bed and breakfast. The business closed in the late 1950s and the building was razed.

BUDD COTTAGE HOTEL
NORTHPORT, MICH.

21097

C. E. SCOTT

Northport, Mich.

Groceries, Confectionery, Cigars

Ice Cream   Baked Goods

Scott Store

Anna and Clarence Scott opened the Scott Store in 1910. The store had a grocery section, a meat counter, a confectionary and an ice-cream parlor. For many years it was a popular spot for locals and tourists alike. In 1936 Elden and Helga Dame purchased the store and it remained a landmark on Nagonaba Street for many years.

THE CEDAR CHEST

Indian Baskets, Moccasins, Souvenirs, Gifts

In Connection with

the Rexall Drug Store

conducted by

R. E. Mervau

Northport,   Michigan

The Cedar Chest

The Cedar Chest was a popular souvenir and gift shop in the mid-twentieth century at the corner of E. Nagonaba and N. Mill Streets. Robert Mervau was the proprietor and sold moccasins, Indian baskets, and Indian jewelry. Other items included Mexican imports, leather souvenirs, and wooden gifts. It operated in connection with the Rexall Drug Store next door.

Within the photo, handwritten:

Indian
CRAFT SHOP

SOUVENIRS
BASKETS
MOCCASINS

GUARANTEED
GENUINE...
Handicraft

Jessie   Lucille

Northports' Indian Craft Shop At M22 & M201 Junction
Prop. Jessie W. Hilton - Grandaughter of Rev. Geo. N. Smith,
Founder of Northport, Mich

Indian Craft Shop

Native Americans found a ready market for their crafts as souvenirs for tourists to bring home. The Indian Craft Shop in Northport offered "guaranteed genuine handicraft" including baskets, birch bark boxes, moccasins and jewelry. The shop was located at the junction of M-22 and M-201. It was operated by Jessie W. Hilton, the granddaughter of Rev. George N. Smith, founder of Northport. Earlier Mrs. Hilton had operated the "Cherry Buttery" featuring her special recipe for cherry butter. Sunday chicken dinners, by reservation only, were cooked on a kerosene stove.

Among the big willows and on the banks of a tumbling stream is

Willow Brook Inn

Famous For Good Food

NORTHPORT   MICHIGAN

Willow Brook Tea Room and Inn

The Willow Brook Inn was opened in 1921 by Bert and Ella Campbell of Chicago. Located along a babbling brook stood a huge willow tree which was the inspiration for the establishment's name. There was a beautiful rock garden and a miniature water wheel on the grounds. The Willow Brook Inn served luncheons, afternoon teas, and special chicken and trout dinners. It also featured homemade cherry pies, cakes, cookies, ice cream and fudge served on a delightful screened-in porch. The homelike surroundings offered comfortable wicker furniture and a charming fieldstone fireplace. The Inn also had rooms for overnight guests. The Campbells operated the summer inn until their deaths in a tragic automobile accident. The Inn was closed for several seasons, but then taken over by their daughter, Marjorie Harbaugh and her husband Roy in 1947. The business changed hands several times over the following years. An advertisement from 1950 stated that the Willow Brook Inn was "recommended by Duncan Hines." The Inn closed in the mid-1960s, but has seen new life as an ice cream parlor in more recent years.

"Open Hearth" Fountain & Grill
Northport, Mich. On M-22.

Open Hearth

The Open Hearth Fountain and Grill opened in 1948 and operated into the mid-1950s. It was located in a building that formerly housed the Village Shops on the northwest corner of Mill and Third Streets. It was owned by Ida Dame and Hattie Steele, who were both good cooks. They served light lunches and fountain confections, and were especially known for their pies and donuts. The "Open Hearth" refers to the prominent fieldstone fireplace, a symbol of welcome and warmth. Note that these postcards incorrectly state the restaurant was on M-22. It was actually located on M-201.

"Open Hearth" Fountain & Grill.
Northport, Mich. On M-22.

HOMEWOOD COTTAGES,
NORTHPORT, MICH. 450-B

The Homewood

"The Homewood - on M-22 in Northport, your home away from home, open year round, 4 cottages and overnight cabins, sleeping 4-6 people. Free TV. Rooms available in Home. Trailer Park. Laundry-mat. $6-$12 per night. Ray and Hilda Lemcool, Northport, Phone EV-6-4161."

-Beautiful Leelanau County, circa 1965

THE

HOMEWOOD COTTAGES

Modern Housekeeping
Cottages

Laundry-mat
Open 24 hours
Attendant Service
Eight 'til Five

TRAILER ACCOMMODATIONS

OPEN YEAR 'ROUND

NORTHPORT
EV 6-4161

GARTHES LOG CABIN ON THE BLUFFS   NORTHPORT, MICH. N 108

Log Cabin at the Bluffs

The Log Cabin at the Bluffs was located two and a half miles west of Northport on a bluff overlooking Lake Michigan. It was built in 1919-1920 by the Garthe family. The building took the shape of a cross, with three areas for eating and one for the kitchen. The kitchen proved to be too small, so a larger kitchen and a living room were added the following year. The restaurant was a family affair, with several members of the family helping out, but the "Misses Garthe" were the mainstays. Meals were by reservation only. Chicken and fish dinners were the house specialties. The chicken was fried, then baked. There was always homemade soup, bread and rolls, cake or fruit pies. Fresh fruits and vegetables were procured from the Garthe's adjoining farm. The cooking and baking were done on a wood stove. The Log Cabin at the Bluffs was an institution in the Northport area and it was a sad day for hungry diners when the restaurant closed in 1953.

GARTHE'S LOG CABIN

PETERSON PARK NORTHPORT, MICH.

Peterson Park

"Summer picnic enthusiasts in Northport needn't go far in search of an ideal place to practice outdoor cookery, for Peterson Park now boasts two newly completed stone fireplaces, in addition to the two already there.... The four convenient outdoor grills with picnic tables close by and a pump for fresh water are set in the midst of a peaceful, scenic spot. Located about three miles northeast of town, the park has a lake view which also includes the Manitou Islands, Fox Islands, and Beaver Island.

The land for Peterson Park was once part of the farm of Hans Peterson, and was presented to the township in his memory by his daughter, Mrs. Anne Peterson Raymond."

-*Northport Tribune*, July 3, 1947

Postcard message:

Tues.
Hi - Weather still good. Yesterday went hunting blue stones. Got quite a few and some Petoskeys too. We will come home Fri. See you then -
                    Virginia, John & Sandy

Postmarked Leland, date not legible
Mailed to Marion, Ohio

PETERSON PARK HIGH BANKS, NORTHPORT, MICH.

The Air Port Ac RTH PORT. Mich   H68

Woolsey Airport

The Clinton Woolsey Airport is located just north of Northport. The airport is named for Captain Woolsey who lost his life in 1927 on a good will flight for the U.S. Government in South American. Woolsey was 32 years old and left a wife and two daughters. He was buried with full military honors in his hometown of Northport. His father, Byron Woolsey, gave 80 acres of his farmland to Leelanau Township as a site for an airport in memory of his son. The township added 120 acres and the airport was dedicated on July 14, 1935. The stone building on the grounds of the airport was originally the site of the Woolsey family's Golden Rod Dairy, where milk and cream were sterilized and bottled for delivery to Northport Point.

C-3157
The Air Port. Northport Mich

Grand Traverse Lighthouse, Northport, Mich.

Flower Urn - Grand Traverse Light House - Cat Head Point Mich 88.

Grand Traverse Lighthouse

The Grand Traverse Lighthouse, sometimes referred to as Cat's Head Light, was built in 1858. The two-story brick building, which housed the keeper and his family, was capped with a small tower that held a Fourth Order Fresnel lens. The lighthouse operated until 1972 when an automatic light tower was erected. Now a museum, it has been carefully restored and decorated with historical artifacts. The grounds are beautifully maintained with flowering shrubs. Stone planters, filled with summer flowers, were hand-crafted by James McCormick, the lighthouse keeper in the 1920s and 1930s. The Fog Signal Building houses maritime exhibits. The lighthouse is located inside the Leelanau State Park, but is operated and maintained by the Grand Traverse Lighthouse Museum.

Light house Park. Northport. Mich.

Postcard message:

Glory-
We are on a little trip in Northern Michigan. Having a good time only tired.
Look on the map where we are - very far north. All OK.   *-Dora*

Postmarked Northport, 1958
Mailed to Jackson, Michigan

LIGHTHOUSE PARK
NORTHPORT, MICH. N109

Leelanau State Park
(formerly Lighthouse Park)

In 1932 the federal government gave the Michigan Department of Conservation just over 30 acres of land reserved for the lighthouse at the tip of the Leelanau peninsula. This became the short-lived Northport State Park. The land was cleared of trees. Picnic tables, toilets and a fireplace were built, and hiking trails were created. Some of the work was done by the W.P.A. during the Great Depression. In 1947 the State determined that the site was too small for a state park, and turned the property over to Leelanau Township for a term of 99 years. The park then became known as Lighthouse Park.

It was turned back to the State of Michigan in 1974 because of the expense of maintaining the park. It was then designated as the Leelanau State Park. The State had started purchasing land near the park in the 1960s with the idea of future expansion. More land was purchased in the 1970s once the state park was established. The park now contains 1,300 acres with a northern section at the tip of the peninsula, and another section of parkland on the western shore of Cathead Bay, about four miles south of the original park. The Grand Traverse Lighthouse Museum lies within the park's boundary.

DINING ROOM RAFFS DEEP SEA FISHING RESORT

C 3065

Chief A Cabin Boat at Raffs Mackanaw Trout Camp Northport Mich N 19

Raff's Fishing Camp

"Raff's camp is the pioneer among the trolling camps for deep sea Mackinaw Trout. Here you will find by far the largest number of easy riding, comfortable cabin cruisers and the best Camp from every point of view of any on the Great Lakes. By long experience, Raff's Camp has the most competent guides and the very cream of the trolling grounds are within three minutes from the dock.

Our camp is easily accessible as good roads lead right up to the camp. State Highway M-22 leads from Traverse City to Northport and our camp is five miles north of the village. An excellent highway [M-22] with beautiful seascapes can be taken all the way from Traverse City....

Our large dining room overlooking the water is a splendid place for wholesome, well-cooked meals famous throughout this entire northern district. Prices are as low as anywhere in Michigan. Four people can fish for $7.50 for a half day or $15.00 all day for the party.... We have a very large fleet of boats available with a competent guide for each boat.

We have a splendid supply of overnight cabins situated just off shore among the pines. Cabins are equipped with electric light and restful beds with innerspring mattresses. Beautiful, sparkling, clean bathing beach in front of our camp. Stay a few days - we'll pack your day's catch in ice for you."

-Raff's Mackinaw Trolling Camp, circa 1935

THE "LUCKY" RETURNING TO DOCK   NELSONS FISHING CAMP
NORTHPORT, MICH.   N 105

Nelson's Mackinaw Trout Trolling Camp

"Enjoy Michigan's greatest outdoor sport. You will need occasional recreation and time to fill your lungs with clean Lake Michigan air to better perform your DEFENSE work.

Nature made her supreme contribution to the health and happiness of mankind when she stocked the waters with game fish - and man's struggle with the hook and line has gone on ever since.

Nature was doubly good to the Northport Region when she created the deep channel home for the fighting Mackinaw Trout - and man has been enjoying the battle of the shinning spinner versus the Mackinaws since the days of the Indians. It continues to offer the thrill of sport fishing combined with healthful, restful recreation so necessary to relieve the tenseness of war times....

Every cabin cruiser at Nelson's is a new vessel, recently constructed. All equipment furnished and of the very best. Comfortable chairs, and toilet facilities on each boat.... Our boats are of ample size to accommodate the entire family and any two of the party can fish at the same time. Women and children enjoy fishing as well as the men.... The thrill of fighting a Mackinaw Trout is a thrill you will long remember.

Excellent roads - scenic highways through Traverse City, north on M-22 to Northport ."

-*Nelson's Mackinaw Trolling Camp*, circa 1944

Cherry Home

Cherry Home was started by Herbert Boughey and Gilman Dame when they bought 200 acres of land about three miles south of Cathead Bay, north of Northport. In the first two years, 1912-13, they planted approximately 14,000 Montmorency cherry trees. Additional land was purchased later and more trees were planted, making a total of 15,000 trees. At one time Cherry Home had 1,000 acres of cultivated cherry trees. Cherry Home became known as the world's largest red tart cherry orchard. Boughey later sold out to Francis Haserot of Cleveland, who eventually became the head of the operation.

Cherry Home built a deep water dock so fairly large boats could bring supplies in and ship cherries out. A warehouse and cannery were also built close to the water's edge. Boats picked up cherries from Suttons Bay, Omena, Old Mission, and the Manitou Islands. In 1921 the company bought its own boat, the Gilman D., later nicknamed the Bull Moose. The "cherry boat" ran between Grand Traverse Bay and Old Mission. Just north of the cannery a store and post office were built. "Cherry Home" became a geographical place name and had its own post office from 1919 through 1931.

In the first years harvesting was done by local folks and teenage boys and girls from Grand Rapids. Later on migrant workers arrived in Northport as seasonal help. During WWII Jamaican workers were employed. Workers lived in dormitories with dining facilities. Some of the dormitories had been barracks at Fort Custer during WWI and were shipped to Northport and hauled out on sleighs to Cherry Home in 1921.

After severe storm damage to the dock and cannery in 1927-28, the company decided to build a new modern canning factory in the village of Northport. In 1929 the first crop was processed in the new plant which had a capacity for canning and freezing several million pounds of red tart and sweet cherries each season. Cherries were also processed for juice. The new factory continued to provide a dormitory and dining room for the workers. Sometimes as many as 125 people were employed during the cherry season in July and August. A former worker remembered that prices for harvesting cherries varied over the years, from a low of 10 cents per lug in 1932 to a high of $1 per lug in 1945.

After WWII the canning factory was remodeled and modernized. It processed 4 million pounds of fruit in 1948. The factory also processed strawberries, apples, peaches, plums, and pears. When 100 acres of old non-producing trees were pulled out, Cherry Home planted asparagus for canning. In the mid-1960s nearly all of the Cherry Home property along the bay was sold to the American Central Corporation which developed the "Cherry Home" subdivision. In 1965 lots starting at $1,195 were advertised for sale. In 1970 an investment firm from Washington D.C. purchased the canning factory and Cherry Home orchards from the Haserot Company, but decided not to continue the business. The orchards and farm land were sold to private parties. The factory was purchased in 1977 by the village of Northport and the old canning factory site is now the Francis H. Haserot Park.

Unloading Cherries at the Canning Factory North Port Mich 134.

Camp Caho

"In the pine woods of Michigan, and on the sheltered bay of the open waters of Lake Michigan lies Camp Caho. One hundred and fifty acres of woodland and shore line are owned by the camp.... With the advantages of a large body of water, and a country noted for its summering opportunities, Caho has an invaluable privacy, and is conveniently apart from the rest of the world.

In years gone by this land was a wilderness.... Now the Caho girls live and grow in this environment. The forests and the sandy shores retain their primal freshness, while to the healthy life of the woods and water are joined the comforts and amenities of modern living....

Life at camp is up-building. It produces the beauty of health and the inner grace, and balance with which this is accompanied. Each day is filled with new experiences, with the life that every girls enjoys, with the events and accomplishments that stimulate self-reliance and develop individuality....

Camp Caho activities are many - for the outdoors, horseback riding, swimming, canoeing, golf, target-practice, hiking, and camping on trip days. Every afternoon for an hour or so after dinner, there is a period of rest. In the evening there is singing at the Log and the pleasures of an open fireplace and good companionship.... 'Something different' in camp activities consists of learning to drive a Ford. Each season a group of girls is given the opportunity to learn to drive the camp Fords and advance through the season until they are rated as Class A drivers - competent to extricate themselves from such difficulties as may arise."

-*Camp Caho,* circa 1925

Shady Trails Camp

Shady Trails, the National Speech Improvement Camp, was founded in 1932 by John and Grace Clancy of Traverse City. The Clancys leased the vacant Indian Beach Lodge, located south of Northport, and opened the camp for boys with only four campers. By 1943 the enrollment had grown to 47 and the campers lived in tents. In 1947 the camp was moved to its new location on M-22 on the shore of Grand Traverse Bay, north of Omena. The 26-acre property had a main lodge, several small cottages and other buildings that served as many as 84 boys. In 1949 the University of Michigan purchased the camp through a donation by the Kresge Foundation. The camp was officially designated as the "University of Michigan Speech Improvement Camp," but the popular name of "Shady Trails Camp" continued to be used. Enrollment grew to about 100 boys each season.

The camp integrated traditional summer camping activities with remedial instruction. Speech, language, reading and hearing therapies were focused on the individual needs of the students. The boys participated in baseball, volleyball, tennis, archery, swimming, fishing, boating, hiking, and other group activities.

The 1994 season saw the last group of campers, and the camp was officially closed in 1995. A new owner purchased the camp, kept the name "Shady Trails Camp," and converted it into a day camp for boys and girls between the ages of five and fourteen.

Northport Point

Northport Point is a narrow strip of densely wooded land projecting into Grand Traverse Bay, just north of the village of Northport. The cottage colony is the site of many magnificent summer homes. In the 1920s it had the distinction of having more "money invested per capita" than any other summer colony in Michigan. Many of the wealthy summer resorters would stay at Northport Point for the season, bringing servants, nannies and cooks with them.

Postcard message:

My Dear Mary,
My but I wish you could be here with us. We are always doing something, like going on hay rides, little kind of party after dinner and such things. Hope you come up with Stanley.
-Margaret

Postmarked Northport Point, date not legible
Mailed to Cincinnati, Ohio

Postcard message:

Hello to all the family-
Am growing fat and lazy - we ride in a dandy motor boat, bathe, walk, eat and sleep each day, so you see it is all play and no work. The evenings are very cool and fine. Hope you are having better weather.
-Lovingly, Marion

Postmarked Northport, 1916
Mailed to Elgin, Ill.

Cedar Lodge

The Cedar Lodge was was built in 1900 on the narrowest part of Northport Point. The rustic lodge built of cedar logs had 50 rooms, all facing the water. The hotel sat on a foundation of cedar posts. The large, open dining room served visitors as well as its guests, and was well known for its cuisine. The hotel was never fancy and furnishings were "summer camp spartan." Bathrooms were located down the hall from the guest rooms.

There was plenty for the Cedar Lodgers to do. There were Saturday night dances, bridge games, bingo, croquet, and occasional magic acts or other entertainment. And, of course, there were all kinds of water activities including bathing, swimming and boating. The Cedar Lodge was razed by a controlled burn in 1960 to make a beach front park for the cottagers.

Postcard message:

You are supposed to sit on this porch and swap fish stories. Jack caught three nice perch yesterday. We wished for you and Grandma when we were eating them tonight.

Love, Constance

Postmark not legible, 1933
Mailed to Waynetown, Indiana

Cherry Basket Fruit Farm
Omena, Mich.

FANCY SWEET CHERRIES

Direct from the Orchard
By Parcel Post

Ready For Shipment About July 15

Cherry Basket Farm

The Cherry Basket Farm, located just north of Omena, was one of many orchards in the M-22 region. However, it was unusual because it was owned and operated by two women, Enid Bailey and Louise Taylor, both from Grand Rapids. Bailey is pictured to the left with her farmhand, Don Inman. The women bought the 86-acre farm in 1926 with only $2,000 down and the balance of $23,500 due in two years. When the women bought the farm, 55 acres were planted in cherries. They had no experience in raising fruit, but through diligent study on the subject and lots of hard work, their first two seasons bore successful crops and they were able to pay off their debt to the bank in only two years time, much to the surprise of the bankers.

The beautiful Cherry Basket gambrel barn was chosen as the 2015 barn of the year by the Michigan Barn Preservation Network.

Oldest Presbyterian Church

The Omena Presbyterian Church, also known as the Grove Hill New Mission Church, is the oldest Presbyterian church north of Grand Rapids. Its white frame building and white spire have the look of churches in New England.

Reverend Peter Dougherty and a band of Ottawas and Chippewas led by Chief Ahgosa moved from the present-day Old Mission Peninsula to the eastern side of the Leelanau Peninsula in 1852. Dougherty established a Presbyterian colony, first calling the settlement New Mission. The church, built and dedicated in 1858, is located on a little hill, just yards from M-22. In the bell tower is the bronze bell which Rev. Dougherty had cast from pennies collected more than a century ago from his congregation. There is a cemetery adjacent to the church where lie the bodies of pioneers and Native Americans who helped to found this quaint village. Since the 1880s, the church has been used mostly in the summer. It remains relatively unchanged from its earliest days. The church is designated as a Michigan State Historic Site and listed on the National Register of Historic Places.

Presbyterian Church. Omena. Mich.

Omena, Mich.

Omena

    The village of Omena is located on the shores of Omena Bay between Northport and Suttons Bay. The name of the settlement, first called New Mission, was changed to Omena in 1858 when a post office was established. Reverend Peter Dougherty was the first postmaster. O-me-nah is a Native American word meaning, "is that so?" Tradition has it that the name came from Reverend Dougherty's habitual response to statements made by Native Americans.

    Omena was the first resort area in Leelanau County. The earliest resorts were Shab-Wah-Sung (later known as the Chicago Club), the Leelanau Hotel, the original Omena Inn, the Clovers and the Sunset Lodge, all opening before 1900. Summer cottages and more resorts were built and Omena became a tourist haven. The early resorters came by ship to Omena's docks. The railroad came in 1903 and made two stops in Omena. The livelihood of many of the local families was sustained by serving the needs of the summer vacationers.

M-22 through Omena

As automobiles became the dominant form of transportation, more vacationers found their way to Omena on M-22. The scenic highway curves along the east side of the Leelanau Peninsula near Omena presenting views of the beautiful bay waters from many spots. M-22 runs through the center of the charming village, which still holds allure for travelers today.

Postcard message:

Dear Martha,
Just a card to let you know I have not forgotten you. I am having such a good time this summer up in Michigan. It is so nice and cool. I wish you could be here. We are coming home the first of Sept. Will see you in school.

-Mary

Postmarked Omena, 1940
Mailed to Kansas City, Kansas

You Can Do Better at

ANDERSON'S

OMENA

Anderson's Store and Ice Cream Parlor

A.F. Anderson founded Anderson's General Store in 1883. A few years he had a new competitor just down the street when Paul Bath opened his general store. Anderson's was a more "modern" store than Barth's and tried to keep up with the changing demands of the public. The store sold a wide variety of items, including groceries, meats, hardware items, paint, agricultural implements, feed and coal. In the early years the store also housed the post office. In the 1920s the store sold gasoline, oil and tires. Besides serving local families and farmers living in the area, the store catered to the burgeoning summer population. In 1947 the Andersons sold the store to Beatrice and Miles Kimmerly, but remained as landlords. The store closed in 1958 and then changed hands several times before David and Sally Viskochil bought the building in 1976 and opened the Tamarack Craftsmen Gallery.

In 1890 the Anderson family opened an ice cream parlor, which was located in the present day post office building. This became a popular spot during the summer in the days before air-conditioning. The store also served as the post office in the busy summer months. Besides ice cream concoctions, the ice cream parlor sold candy and soda pop, Indian baskets, postcards and tourist items.

Putnam's Texaco Gas Station

As more and more automobiles came on the scene, the need for gasoline and automotive services increased and a new business model was created. In 1935 John Putnam built Omena's third gas station in a small building on M-22 across from Anderson's general store. There he sold Texaco gasoline. Business was good and three years later he added a service bay for mechanical work and a bar with seating for about 30 people. He also built living quarters facing the bay.

The Harbor Bar

In 1957 John Putnam sold his gas station to Keith Brown who enlarged the building and expanded the dining area to accommodate up to 150 customers. Brown fittingly named the business the Harbor Bar because of the expansive view of Omena Bay from the Bar's interior. He added gas pumps to the newly created marina, but soon concentrated more on food and beverages than gasoline, using the slogan, "Have a brew while you enjoy our view." With the success of the restaurant, Brown ended the automotive services in 1981. The building has since changed hands several times.

The Clovers

The Clovers was one of Omena's early hotels. It was situated on a slight elevation overlooking Grand Traverse Bay about a mile south of Omena on M-22. So named because of its spread of fragrant clover blossoms, the 22-acre resort included a main building, and three other houses that combined could accommodate 75 guests. Sidney Keyes started the resort in 1898. He sold the property to Wilberforce and Eliza Foltz in 1911, and it stayed in the Foltz family until 1936. The Clovers continued to flourish under its later owners, the Steins and then the Ermans. The resort closed in 1955 and remained vacant for almost two decades. In the early 1970s it was operated as a commune called the "Manna House." In 1980 it was condemned and burned.

In the early days before M-22 reached the resort, vacationers came by steamship with boats stopping three times a day so travelers could make connections with trains in Traverse City. When the railroad came through Omena in 1903, the Clovers had its own station. The hotel was very fashionable in its early days, with fine furnishings, a grand piano and artwork on display. Guests dressed for dinner every night. The dining room could seat 100 people. Dinners were served to both the Clovers' guests and to vacationers in the area. The resort had its own farm and served fresh vegetables and fruit from its orchard of 200 trees. The Clovers had its own dairy cows for fresh country milk and butter, and chickens for eggs.

Many of the first resorters coming to the Clovers stayed for weeks or for the whole season. By the 1920s, vacationers coming by automobile tended to stay for a shorter time, brought less luggage, and didn't necessarily dress formally for dinner every night. The Clovers adapted to the new wave of vacationers and advertised "to the city dweller and especially the office worker in the city" that what they needed was a complete change of environment. The Clovers could provide rest and relaxation away from the "noise, crowds, hurry and high pressure life of the metropolis."

Omena Bay Lodge, Omena, Mich.

Omena Bay Lodge
(formerly The Oaks)

Located on Omena Point overlooking Grand Traverse Bay just off M-22, the Omena Bay Lodge started its life as the Oaks Hotel. Originally built as a private cottage, it was sold to Benjamin H. Grierson, who renovated the cottage and took on "paying guests." It became known as "The Oaks." In 1913 new owners enlarged the frame house into a hotel and added its signature two-story porch. Various proprietors managed the hotel over the next two decades. In 1935 Hector and Jessie Carmichael of Chicago purchased the hotel and changed the name to the "Omena Bay Lodge." They renovated the hotel, added running water to every guest room and installed innerspring mattresses on the beds. The rates in 1935 for the Omena Bay Lodge were $5.00 a day, American Plan, with three daily meals provided. By the late 1940s the Carmichaels had sold the property and the new owners changed the name to "Omena Point Lodge." They advertised in 1949 for people to "Visit Our Flowing Sulphur Artesian Well."

In its heyday the hotel boasted that it offered visitors "everything for a pleasant summer vacation." Its shaded woodlands were endowed with walking and bridle paths. One mile of bay frontage offered private bathing beaches and a dock with "runabouts for excursions on the bay." Fishing trips for Mackinaw Trout were arranged by the lodge. There were both cement and clay tennis courts, and golf courses in the vicinity. Like many of the old hotels around the state, changing tastes led to its decline. The hotel burned down about 1950.

Sunset Lodge Omena, Mich.

Sunset Lodge

The Sunset Lodge, situated on a bluff overlooking Grand Traverse Bay, has been a fixture in Leelanau County since 1898 when it was built by Leonard and Rhoda Wheeler. It remained in the family for almost 80 years. The Wheeler's three-story house, built as their retirement home for their "sunset" years, became a thriving resort business. They added two cottages about 1905, which looked like houses, had indoor plumbing and finished walls, and were habitable year round. Later additions included a dining room and social hall, a summer kitchen and a barn for the horses and carriages. Tennis courts and croquet grounds were installed. The resort continued to undergo changes over the years, but always kept its charm and home-like atmosphere. The dining room could seat 100 people and the reputation for good food brought nearby cottagers besides the Sunset's guests. The large parlor and library served as a gathering place for lively discussions and games of charades. In the early days, local fiddlers played occasional dances in the social hall. A radio was later purchased to provide music, and for a few years, college musicians were hired to play live music.

The Sunset Lodge managed to survive through the Great Depression, WWII and the changing travel habits of the public. While other hotels of the resort era are long gone, the Sunset Lodge still maintains most of its original buildings and still welcomes visitors to Leelanau County as a bed and breakfast.

Sunset Lodge Omena, Mich.

Omena Inn

The Omena Inn was built in 1858 as the manse for Reverend Peter Dougherty, one of Omena's prominent early settlers. When the Doughertys left Omena in 1871, the building served as a summer home for 50 years for several different owners. In 1920 John and Frances Santo bought the house and adjoining property and transformed the home into the Omena Inn, adding many features in the Craftsman style which was popular at the time. They expanded the home with two side wings that nearly doubled the size. They added the stately stone porch columns which supported a screened-in second-story porch. There was a large sitting room, lounge, recreation room and private dining room. The main dining room was located on the southern side of the building, tastefully decorated with each table "sporting snowy linen and shiny service." The second floor held guest rooms with baths, electric lights, and "lathed, plastered and papered" walls.

In 1931 the Inn was sold to Charles and Theresa "Sweetie" Cordray. Sweetie was a great cook and her Sunday dinners attracted local folks as well as the Inn's guests. In 1943 the Inn was sold again. Two couples, Albert and Lillian Landis and Abraham and Jennie Soifers made the purchase. Under their reign the Inn's employees put on live entertainment for the guests. The Inn changed hands over the next several years. Its days as an inn ended in the early 1960s when Dr. Joseph Melton opened Camp Omena. After falling into disrepair, the Inn was purchased in 1978 by Walter and Beverly Gaudette, who upon learning of the building's history, restored it to its original footprint. The building remains in private hands.

Omena Inn, Omena Mich.

Porch, Beautiful Omena Inn, Omena, Mich.

Postcard message:

The pavilion at Omena Point. Did a LOT of dancing there during the summer of 1921. Thoroughly enjoyed the summer even tho I had to work hard. Worked at "The Oaks."

Postcard not mailed

Yacht Club

In 1911 the Omena Pavilion on the shore of Omena Bay was built as a community center to provide diversions for residents, local farmers, and summer resorters and their staffs. Membership for families was $10 a year. Saturday nights were open for non-members, and intended primarily for summer employees "who should have recreation as well." Dances became a regular feature. The pavilion also featured occasional vaudeville acts or musical performances. Through the rough years of Prohibition, the Great Depression and WWII the pavilion lay dormant.

In 1948 the Omena-Traverse Yacht Club was established. Fundraising efforts allowed the group to purchase the neglected pavilion building one year later. The Yacht Club organized regular boating activities and occasional regattas. The Club continued the tradition of providing diversions for Omena people with dances, themed-parties and Venetian nights.

Solle's Bookstore

ALL THE WORLD
Comes to
SOLLE'S BOOK SHOP
In Person or by Mail. A Big City Bookshop Where All Roads End.
OMENA — MICHIGAN

Omena, Mich.

Postcard message:

We were at a bookstore at Omena and we had a great feast of books. You would enjoy it I am sure. Will tell you more later.

-Chas.

Postmarked Suttons Bay, 1945
Mailed to Rockford, Michigan

"It is a strange little shop that Will Solle runs. It's out in the country on the way to Northport, and a plain sign beside the road announces it…. After four years in business here in the north woods, it has become a national institution. Everywhere, the world over, where book collectors gather, the name of Solle is becoming known. His catalog, printed on a little press in the attic … now goes out to regular customers in 42 states and half a dozen countries…. And one day last week the customers who found their way up the winding dirt path to his door, set down their home addresses in the register as Illinois, Texas, New York, Indiana, Ohio, California, Tennessee, London, England, and the island of Majorca.

Solle is a quiet, bookish-looking man who came north for his health half a dozen years ago, after being the ace salesman in one of Chicago's most prosperous book stores…. He brought his personal library of several thousand volumes with him, and settled down in the rented little farmhouse to get back his strength. And as times began to pinch, he offered his books for sale…. That was the beginning of his bookshop in the woods. Now he has 3,000 volumes on his shelves, and does a large mail order business….

The wrens keep trying to nest in his shelves of Michigan authors, the field mice try to sneak in with the customers, and the chipmunks let their curiosity overcome their caution, and come up to the door. Solle finds the Omena woods quite different from Chicago's Michigan boulevard."

-*Grand Rapids Press,* September 14, 1936

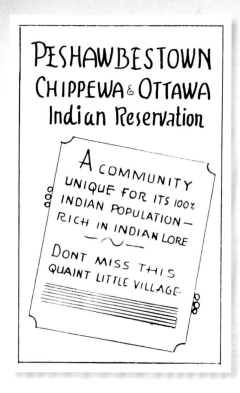

Peshawbestown

The village of Peshawbestown, located between Omena and Suttons Bay, was known as Eagletown until sometime in the 1880s. Legend tells that it was named for an eagle's nest high in a pine tree near the old Indian trail. The trail, later called the Peshawbestown Road, now has given way to M-22, which goes through the heart of the village.

The name Peshawbestown is said to be named after Chief Peshawbe, who is believed to have migrated to the area from Cross Village about 1852. Some scholars date the arrival of the Ottawa band to the 1840s.

The U.S. Government recognized the Grand Traverse Reservation in 1855. A church was built in 1858 a little to the south of the present one. It was later replaced by a frame structure which burned, leaving only the sacristy standing. The present church was built about 1865 using the old sacristy. The church was first referred to as the Indian Mission Church, later as the Immaculate Conception Church, but is now called the Blessed Kateri Tekakwitha Church. A school was built in 1861 and was used to teach the local Native American children until 1941 when it burned. A cemetery on the church grounds holds the remains of early settlers in the area.

By 1870 the Grand Traverse Reservation had the largest number of Native Americans in the area, with some living at Eagletown and others living at Leland, Cat Head Point, Northport, Omena and Suttons Bay. In 1934 an effort was made under the Indian Reorganization Act to seek federal recognition as a tribe, but was denied, as was another attempt in 1943. A final effort brought federal recognition in 1980 to the Grand Traverse Band of Ottawa and Chippewa Indians, acknowledging them as a self-governing nation.

The Super Bingo Palace, which opened in 1984, developed into the Leelanau Sands Casino, which was the first tribal casino to open in the United States. The band opened the Eyaawing Museum in Peshawbestown in 2009 and has an annual pow wow every summer to celebrate its heritage.

The name of the village has undergone several spellings over the years, including Peshabatown, Peshabetown and Pshawbatown.

Peshawbestown Centennial

The Peshawbestown centennial celebration was held on August 30, 1947. It marked the founding of the Native American settlement in 1845 with a plaque placed on a monument stone in front of the Indian Mission Church (now the Blessed Kateri Tekakwitha Church). The keynote speaker was Congressman Albert J. Engel, representative of the Ninth Congressional District. A ceremonial dance was performed by the local Native Americans to mark the occasion.

CHURCH AT PESHAWBESTOWN, MICH. N 200

Reviving Handicrafts

In the mid-1960s there was a resurgence of interest in traditional Native American crafts. A revival of the skills of making baskets, birch bark items and other handicrafts was underway. There was also a newfound interest in the traditional dances and games of the Ottawa and Chippewa tribes of Michigan.

Teaching the younger generation the traditional skills of their ancestors was the only way to keep the artistry alive. There was much skill and knowledge involved. The proper materials had to be found. Black Ash, even back in the 1960s, was getting scarce. The trees had to be cut in the month of June and the logs had to be pounded with a mallet until the annual growth rings broke apart. The strips then had to be divided into the correct sizes for basket weaving and scraped with a sharp knife. Once the splints were cut to size, they were dyed and ready to be woven into baskets.

Interest in Native American crafts has continued to grow in the last several decades and Native American artists are emerging with new enthusiasm for the traditions and skills practiced by the preceding generations.

Materials Found in Nature

Susan Pequongay of Peshawbestown was one of the talented Native Americans to carry on the crafts of her ancestors. Using materials found in nature, the artist created beautiful little boxes. The containers were made from porcupine quills and birch bark. Birch bark is cut from trees in May and June, when the sap is abundant and cutting off the outer bark will not cause harm to the tree. The art of decorating birch boxes with porcupine quills is unique to North America. Making such decorative containers is a time consuming and meticulous operation. Quills must be collected in January and February when their color is the most vivid and they are less oily. One porcupine can provide 30,000 to 40,000 quills, ranging in length up to five inches. Quilling requires strong hands, careful attention to detail and much patience. Today these magnificent boxes are highly collectible.

Postcard message:

Cherry Cove Beach-
Sun, sand, water - and no concept of time, except that this won't go on much longer. Cooler today but that
doesn't keep the children off the beach. We've already made our annual trip to the Dunes - up, down and
around. Haven't driven "North of Suttons Bay" yet, but will make the trip in a day or so. Best wishes.
- Muriel, Jerry & the children

Postmarked Suttons Bay, 1954
Mailed to Grosse Pte. Farms, Michigan

Suttons Bay

Located between Northport and Traverse City, the village of Suttons Bay faces eastward toward the bay of the same name. It was settled in 1854 when Harry C. Sutton arrived with a crew of woodsmen to set up a wooding station for supplying cordwood to passing steamboats. Originally called Suttonsburg, the name had been changed to Pleasant City in an effort to attract more residents. That effort failed and in 1861 when the first post office was established, the village became Suttons Bay.

Lumbering became the predominant industry, followed later by cherry cultivation and tourism. The town's population grew and the village was incorporated in 1898. The railroad came to Suttons Bay in 1903. Soon after, the stagecoach routes were eliminated and the Traverse Bay Line of steamers stopped running.

When the automobile came on the scene, commerce expanded and made the village a regional center of trade. M-22 brought a new wave of vacationers to Suttons Bay seeking its natural beauty, recreational opportunities and cultural activities. Today Suttons Bay's history lives on in its historic buildings, including the renowned Bay Theater and the venerable Bahle's of Suttons Bay.

The Nation's Playground

"Suttons Bay (population 500) ... situated on M-22, the famed, 'Manitou Trail,' is easy to reach - just 20 miles from Traverse City.... The pace is leisurely, the setting uncommercialized and of outstanding scenic beauty. The countryside is rolling hills, whose sunny slopes produce some of the world's finest cherry orchards. Suttons Bay is alive with activity during the colorful cherry harvest in July and August.... Resort facilities are all about. Hotels, furnished cottages, tourist rooms, trailer parking - take your choice.... Recreations include swimming, beach playgrounds, sailing, motor boating, water skiing, excellent fishing, tennis, with other sports near at hand. Church, library, and movie theatre welcome summer visitors. Artists and camera fans find a wealth of interesting material for canvas and lens. Health advantages of Suttons Bay have long been recognized. Surrounded by large bodies of water, the air is pure and practically free from pollen, appreciated by hay fever patients."

-Suttons Bay, Leelanau County, 1954

A Welcoming Community

Suttons Bay has a long reputation for welcoming visitors to "Leelanau County's Trading Center." In early promotional materials the village boasted of its bustling business community and good fellowship. Its busy trading center welcomed summer visitors and local folks alike, claiming that Suttons Bay's stores were noted for their low prices on quality merchandise. An ad from 1929 proclaimed "We don't try to Jesse James the Resorter. We want them to come back."

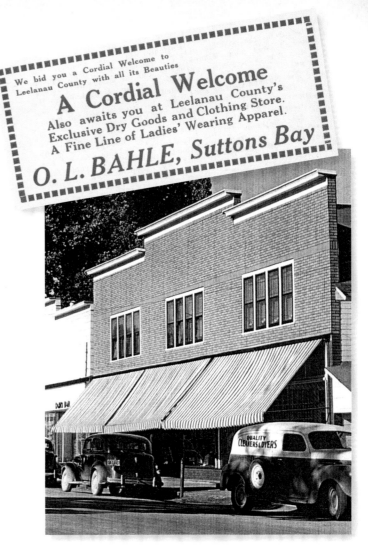

Bahle's

Bahle's is one of the oldest businesses in Suttons Bay. Established by Lars Bahle in 1876, it is still a vibrant enterprise today. The store persists as one of the few Michigan businesses founded and operated by the same family for over 135 years. A general store approach worked in the early years, but today the store focuses on classic fine clothing for men and women.

Fieldstone Buildings

Fieldstone buildings were fairly common in northern Michigan. The material was locally available, inexpensive and rugged. The two-story stone Union School was built in 1907. Local farmers hauled wagon loads of unwanted stones from their fields to the Lincoln Street site. The building was used as a school until 1968. In the 1970s Frigid Foods used the building as a dormitory for employees. The kitchen was used to prepare hundreds of meals for the Frigid Food workers until the mid-1980s. The beautiful stone building was then used as a bed and breakfast for a few years, but now consists of privately owned condominiums.

The Suttons Bay depot was completed in 1920 by the Leelanau Transit Company, which leased the railroad line to the Manistee and Northeastern Railroad. The depot is a single-story, Arts-and-Crafts style structure with a hip roof and overhanging eaves. The tracks north of Suttons Bay were abandoned in the 1960s. The Leelanau Scenic Railroad used the depot and the tracks south of Suttons Bay for excursions from 1989 until 1995. The tracks were removed in 1996 when construction of the Leelanau Trail began. The building was listed on the National Register of Historic Places in 1997 and is now home to a regional law firm.

Rustic Tea Room

"What is fast proving a popular rendezvous for the hordes of summer visitors who annually come to this region is the rustic tea room here, recently opened by two college girls, the Misses Nellie Bahle and Ruth Solem. It's a place where one can stop and have a piece of home-made pie, a chicken sandwich, or a whole chicken roast for that matter, while his engine is cooling....

Designed and constructed by Carl Garthe, local builder, the building is a thing to inspire the artist. Its quaint rustic outside is distinctly of the north. Small and straight cedar sapling trunks form both frame and wall completing a suggestion of the eighteenth century stockade of pioneer days and still possessing enough of the atmosphere of the twentieth century to let you know you are in touch with modern civilization.

The roof is low, almost flat, and seems to squat over the rest of the structure in the manner a mother hen does her chicks. Truly, the roof seems to spread the invitation of hospitality. The furnishings of the quaint structure harmonize with the outside, except that a suggestion of the mystic is rendered at night when dozens of Japanese paper lanterns shed their glow over the place....

Both Miss Bahle and Miss Solem are modest as to their accomplishments and it is with difficulty that one would learn the source of their inspiration for running a tea room. It seems that each had gained the name of being a culinary artist long before the thought of going into business was entertained. And it was only after the oft-repeated suggestion on the part of local residents and such resorters as they already knew that they engage in such an enterprise that they determined to do so.

And after a few weeks of experience at satisfying hungry stomachs and cheering travel-worn visitors, the girls decided they like it far beyond their expectations."

-Grand Rapids Herald, July 20, 1924

Vacation Spot

"The breeze, always, 'off the water,' tempers the climate, summer or winter. The air, like the water, is pure and clean.... Miles of clean sandy beaches and sparkling clear water provide hours of healthful fun and relaxation - and the beaches are never crowded. Suttons Bay is the natural center for all your vacation activity, no matter what season. Live comfortably. Everything you could need or want is here."

-Suttons Bay, Leelanau County, 1954

Postcard message:

Hi Folks:
We have had wonderful vacation weather. Harm fishes, the girls swim and sun bathe and I cook meals. We saw the Cherry Festival Parade and it was beautiful. The family leaves Sat. but I'm staying another week to visit with my old college friend.

-Love, Isle

Postmarked Suttons Bay, 1955
Mailed to Grant, Mich.

Sanders Cottages

"Nine miles north of Traverse City, Michigan on State Highway M-22. On the shore of Grand Traverse Bay (Beautiful Leelanau Peninsula). Nine all-new, modern one and two-bedroom cottages. Each cottage on the shore, with large picture window and unobstructed view, private baths with tubs and showers, completely equipped kitchens, safe, sandy beach. No pets allowed. For reservations write George A. Sanders, Suttons Bay, or phone I-3560."

-postcard back, circa 1965

Postcard message:

Hi there Pal,
Oh such a wonderful trip & ideal weather. Yesterday we went
hunting stones. Got about 100 Petoskey stones further north than
where we're staying. We love swimming here. Don't want to go
home.

-Love, Sandy

Postmarked Suttons Bay, 1966
Mailed to Lake City, Michigan

Frigid Foods

Frigid Foods, located just north of Suttons Bay, was a large employer of seasonal workers. As many as 60 to 80 people were hired during the harvest season, including positions from line workers to semi-truck drivers. The company's main business was in canning and freezing strawberries, cherries and apples, but they also took in blueberries, crabapples, elderberries, plums, and other fruit. A station was set up in Bower's Harbor to collect fruit from that area. An advertisement from 1946 invited people to visit the cherry department on the 4th of July. The business was operated for about 30 years before closing in the mid-1980s. Although a subsidiary of Frigid Food Products of Detroit, the plant was a big part of the local community. The company sponsored a local bowling team, provided canned or frozen cherries for a pie-baking contest in Northport during National Cherry Week, and furnished a float in the Cherry Festival parade in Traverse City. The plant was located on the current site of Bayview Condos.

Suttons Bay

Pitted

DARK SWEET PITTED
CHERRIES
IN HEAVY SYRUP
SUTTONS BAY PACKING CO.

VIEW OF GRAND TRAVERSE BAY FROM HY. M 22 SUTTONS BAY, MICH. N 252

Postcard message:

Dear Millie,
Richard and I are having a fine vacation trip. We are touring the Leelanau peninsula and have seen some fine sights. Camped last night in a tourist camp near Suttons Bay and met some folks from Indiana. Heading to Traverse City next. Eating sweet cherries. Will try to bring some back if we don't eat them all!

-Wanda

Postmarked Traverse City, 1941
Mailed to Reed City, Mich.

Greilickville

"The largest community in Leelanau is Greilickville, located at the southeast corner of the county. Almost entirely residential, this community has grown almost fourfold in the last ten years. Named for the Greilick brothers, the area has been variously the site of a prosperous grist mill, brickyard, brewery and sawmill.

Greilickville boasts one of the finest yacht havens and marinas on the Great Lakes. A large township park on the shore of Grand Traverse Bay affords public docking and a modern marina offers every service to the visiting yachtsman. In addition to its own modern shopping center, the community offers the facilities of downtown Traverse City, only a few minutes away."

-Leelanau County Michigan, Land of Delight
Vacation Guide 1961

Ray Darrow's Marina
Featured:

Chris-Craft Boats
Fiber Glass Boats
Aluminum Boats
Freeland Metal Boats
Canoes
Evinrude Motors
Standard Steel Docks
Boat Hoists
Water Skis
Boat Trailers
Boat Cushions
Complete Marine Supplies

Ray Darrow Marine Base

"A brand new modern marina, designed, built and operated by men with a lifetime of experience in the business of boating. A land-locked yacht harbor where every possible service for boats, motors, equipment and electronics can be performed efficiently, quickly and at a reasonable cost.

LOCATION: On the starboard side at lower end of West Arm of Traverse Bay, just inside the Government breakwater, one and a quarter miles NW of Traverse City. Harbor entrance from SE approach.

SERVICES: Fueling and service dock 300 feet long, with water 10 feet deep alongside. Electricity and fresh water outlets. Club facilities with hot showers, restrooms, complete galley, large fireplace and comfortable lounge. No charge for docking first two days.

SUPPLIES: Complete marine supplies and equipment at marina. Supermarkets nearby. Five-minute drive to Traverse City shopping district, with transportation provided or car rental service available.

FACILITIES: Complete marine facilities to handle every possible type of repair; for engine, hull, carpentry, electric or refinishing. 35-ton hoist. Inside and outside storage and summer dockage."

-Vacation Days in Michigan's Grand Traverse Bay Region, 1960

Illustration Credits

Front Cover: Lake Co (IL) Discovery Museum, Curt Teich Postcard Archives, hand-colored by Dianne Carroll Burdick**; Back Cover:** M-22 logo, MDOT; map, Leelanau Historical Society; **ii** MDOT; **iv** Judith Anderson; **vii** Leelanau Historical Society; **viii** MDOT; **1** Omena Historical Society; **2** top, Phil Balyeat; bottom, Empire Area Heritage Group; **3** *Biennial Report of the State Highway Commissioner*, 1913-14; **5** top sign, *Maps, Routes and Tourist's Directory of the West Michigan Pike*, 1914; left & middle signs, created by Rob Burdick based on Michigan State Trunkline signage; far right sign, MDOT; **6 & 7** Leelanau Historical Society; **8** *Emmet County Graphic*, June 9, 1938; **10** Leelanau Historical Society; **11** left, *Benzie County Vacationland*, circa 1955; right ad, *Carefree Days in West Michigan*, 1958; **12** Leelanau Historical Society; **13** left, Phil Balyeat; top ad, *Carefree Days in West Michigan*, 1966; bottom, *Follow the M-22 Portion of the Michigamee Trail*, circa 1966; **14** photo, Leelanau Historical Society; graphic, Michigan Polar-Equator Club; **15** Great Lakes Commission; **16** Networks Northwest; **17** top and right postcards, Phil Balyeat; bottom left, Jack D. Rader; **18** God's Country and Your Vacation - Manistee County; postcards: Lake Co (IL) Discovery Museum, Curt Teich Postcard Archives; **19** *West Michigan Vacation Directory*, 1930; **20** ad, *Carefree Days in West Michigan*, 1962; **23** lower left, Judith Anderson; lower right, *Harmony Camp Tourist Cottages and Cabins*, circa 1930; **24** postcards, Judith Anderson; ad, *Manistee Vacation Guide*, 1939; **25** *Sprenger's Resort Lakeview Hotel*, circa 1930; **26** both right, Judith Anderson; **27** ad, *West Michigan Vacation Directory*, 1925; postcards, Judith Anderson; **28** top right, Judith Anderson left & bottom photos, Camp Tosebo; ad, *Manistee County, Michigan*, 1956; **29** left, *Harmony Camp Tourist Cottages and Cabins*, circa 1930; ad right, *Manistee County, Michigan*, 1952; **30** ad, *Vacation Guide Manistee*, 1945; **32** Lyle Matteson; **33** left, Lyle Matteson; **34 & 35** Arcadia Area Historical Society; **36** middle, Lyle Matteson; bottom, Arcadia Area Historical Society; **38** *Benzie County Fishing and Vacation Guide*, 1940; postcards, Lake Co (IL) Discovery Museum, Curt Teich Postcard Archives; **39** *West Michigan Vacation Directory*, 1930; **40** top, Lyle Matteson; **41** left ad, *Benzie County Fishing and Vacation Guide*, 1941; right ad, *Benzie County Fishing and Vacation Guide*, 1938; postcard, Benzie Area Historical Society; **42** postcards, Benzie Area Historical Society; ad, *Benzie County Fishing and Vacation Guide*, 1940; **43** Grace and Steve Truman; **44** postcards, Benzie Area Historical Society**;** ad, *Winter Sports in West Michigan*, 1954**; 45** top, Benzie Area Historical Society; **46** *Auto Ferry Across Lake Michigan*, 1932; **47** bottom, Bentley Historical Library, University of Michigan; ad, *Benzie County Fishing and Vacation Guide*, 1941; **54,** top ad, *West Michigan Vacation Directory*, 1929; bottom ad, *Benzie County Fishing and Vacation Guide*, 1940; **55** left ad, Congregational Summer Assembly, *In 1948 Vacation with Us*; right postcard, Benzie Area Historical Society, right ad, *Winter Sports in West Michigan*, 1956; **56** Bentley Historical Library, University of Michigan; **57** ad, *Vacation Days in the Grand Traverse Bay Region*, 1946; postcard, Bentley Historical Library, University of Michigan; **60** ad, *Benzie County Fishing and Vacation Guide*, 1941; **61** Benzie Area Historical Society; **63** bottom left, Bentley Historical Library, University of Michigan; **65** bottom, Benzie Area Historical Society; **66** left, Benzie Area Historical Society; **67** Grace and Steve Truman; **69** bottom, Bentley Historical Library, University of Michigan; **70** Chimney Corners; **71** ad, *Benzie County Fishing and Vacation Guide*, 1937; postcard, Benzie Area Historical Society; **72** *D.H. Day State Park/Benzie Unit*, circa 1960; **73** bottom, Bentley Historical Library, University of Michigan; **74** bottom, Benzie Area Historical Society; **75** Archives of Michigan; **76** *Vacation Handbook and Fisherman's Guide Leelanau County*, 1942; **77** *West Michigan Vacation Directory*, 1930; **79 & 80** Empire Area Heritage Group; **81** top, Empire Area Heritage Group; **82** Empire Area Heritage Group; **83** top left, Empire Area Heritage Group; middle & bottom, Jill Cheney; **84** ad, *Road Map and Business Directory of Leelanau County*, circa 1925; photos, Empire Area Heritage Group; **85** ad, *Northport Tribune*, June 30, 1949; pennant & photo, Empire Area Heritage Group; **86** ad, *Vacation Handbook and Fisherman's Guide Leelanau County*, 1938; **87** ad, *Carefree Days in West Michigan*, 1957; **88** top & middle, Empire Area Heritage Group; bottom, Leelanau Historical Society, **89** poster & middle & bottom photos, Empire Area Heritage Group; top photo, Leelanau Historical Society; **91** Grace & Steve Truman; **92** ad, *Leelanau Enterprise*, July 5, 1934; **93** ad, *Road Map and Business Directory of Leelanau County*, circa 1925; top postcard, Empire Area Heritage Group; **94** ad, *Leelanau Enterprise*, July 4, 1929; postcard, National Park Service, Sleeping Bear Dunes National Lakeshore; **95** Empire Area Heritage Group; **97** ad, *Vacation Handbook and Fisherman's Guide Leelanau County*, 1942; photo, Leelanau School Archives; **98** top photo, Empire Area Heritage Group; ad, *West Michigan Vacation Directory*, 1931; **100** *D.H. Day State Park/Benzie Unit*, circa 1960; **101** top left, Empire Area Heritage Group; top right, Jill Cheney; bottom, *D.H. Day State Park/Benzie Unit*, circa 1960; **103** top right, Empire Area Heritage Group; bottom right, George Weeks; **105** top, Grand Rapids Public Library; bottom, Leelanau Historical Society; **106** left photo, Archives of Michigan; **107** top, Jill Cheney; **108**, top, Phil Balyeat; **109** left, Lelanau Historical Society; top right, Phil Balyeat; bottom right, Bentley Historical Library, University of Michigan; **110** Grand Rapids Public Library; **111** top left, Empire Area Heritage Group; top right, *Grand Traverse Region*, 1939; **112** top, Grand Rapids Public Library; **113** ad, *Vacation Handbook and Fisherman's Guide Leelanau County*, 1942; bottom, Empire Area Heritage Group; **114** Grand Rapids Public Library; **115** top, Empire area Heritage Group; bottom, Archives of Michigan; **116** top Archives of Michigan; ad, *Carefree Days in West Michigan*, 1952; **117** Empire Area Heritage Group, photos by Roy Keyoth; **118** Phil Balyeat; **119** sign, Empire Area Heritage Group; photo, Phil Balyeat; **120** ad, *Carefree Days in West Michigan*, 1957; photo, Phil Balyeat, **121** *Sleeping Bear Dunesmobile Scenic Dune Rides*, circa 1959; photos, Phil Balyeat; **122** *Sleeping Bear Dunes Wagon Dune Rides*, circa 1970; **123** Phil Balyeat; **124** Bentley Historical Library, University of Michigan; **125** ad, *CarefreeDays in West Michigan*, 1969; **126** Bentley Historical Library, University of Michigan; **127** MLive Media Group from *The Grand Rapids Press*, November 6, 1977; **128** ad, *Vacation Handbook and Fisherman's Guide Leelanau County*, 1941; top postcard, Lake Co (IL) Discovery Museum, Curt Teich Postcard Archives; **129** ad, *Vacation Handbook and Fisherman's Guide Leelanau County,* 1940; **131** ad, *Leelanau County, Michigan - Land of Delight Vacation Guide 1961*; postcard, Jack D. Rader; **132** postcards, Empire Area Heritage Group; ad, *Leelanau Enterprise,* July 8, 1926; **133** Jill Cheney; **136** top, Leelanau Historical Society; **137** ad, *Vacation Handbook and Fisherman's Guide Leelanau County,* 1938; **139** bottom, Jill Cheney; ad, adapted from 1931 ad by Rob Burdick; **140** top, Empire Area Heritage Group; ad, *Vacation Days in Michigan's Grand Traverse Bay Region,* 1948; **141** ad, *Carefree Days in West Michigan,* 1957; postcard, Empire Area Heritage Group; **142,** ad, *King's Official Route Guide,* 1920; postcard, Empire Area Heritage Group; **143** ad, *Vacation Handbook and Fisherman's Guide Leelanau County,* 1938; bottom, Jill Cheney; **144** top & middle postcards, Empire Area Heritage Group; Hilton ad, *Vacation Handbook and Fisherman's Guide Leelanau County,* 1938; Steffens' ad, *Leelanau Enterprise,* October, 10, 1947; **145** Art's Tavern; **146** top, Empire Area Heritage Group; ad, *Northport Tribune,* August 25, 1949; **147** top postcard, Jill Cheney; ad, *Beautiful Leelanau County,* circa 1965; bottom postcard, Lake Co (IL) Discovery Museum, Curt Teich Postcard Archives; **148** top, Empire Area Heritage Group; **151** flour bag, Leelanau Historical Society; postcard, Empire Area Heritage Group; **152** top photo, Michael Huey/Witt-Dorring Family Archives; bottom, Leelanau School Archive; **153** top, Jill Cheney; **155 & 156** Leelanau School Archives; **157** ad, *Carefree Days in West Michigan,* 1963; **158** ad, *Leelanau Enterprise,* July 4, 1929; **159,** *Vacation Days in Michigan's Grand Traverse Bay Region,* 1963; **161** ad, *Leelanau County, Michigan - Land of Delight Vacation Guide 1961;* **162** ad, adapted from a 1937 ad by Rob Burdick; left postcard, Leelanau Historical Society; **164** Color Postcard Co.; **165** ad, *Carefree Days in West Michigan,* 1957; **167** postcards, Traverse City History Center; ad, *Vacation Days in the Grand Traverse Bay Region,*1946; **168** photos, Phil Balyeat; ad, *Winter Sports in West Michigan,* 1956; **169** Phil Balyeat; **170** top, Color Postcard Co. & Burton Frook Photography; **172** postcards, Leelanau Historical Society; ad, *Vacation Days in the Grand Traverse Bay Region,* 1946; **173** Michigan State University Archives; **174** top, Leelanau Historical Society; ad, *Resort Directory of Leland and Surrounding Region,* 1937; **177** top**,** Leelanau Historical Society; **178** bottom, Grand Rapids Public Library; **179** ad, *Leelanau Enterprise,* July 19, 1934; top photo, Leelanau Historical Society; **180** postcard, Leelanau Historical Society; **181,** Leland Mercantile; **182** ad, *Vacation Handbook and Fisherman's Guide Leelanau County,* 1939; postcard, Leelanau Historical Society; **183** top, Leelanau Historical Society; **184** photo, Leelanau Historical Society; ad, *Leelanau Enterprise,* July 3, 1930; **185** ad, *Northport Leader,* July 29,1926; **186** ad, *Michigan Scenic Highways and Points of Interest,* 1933; **187** ad, *Carefree Days in West Michigan,* 1946; **189** top, Leelanau Historical Society; **190** ad, *Northport Leader,* July 29, 1926; postcard, Leelanau Historical Society; **191** photos, Fischer's Happy Hour Tavern; ad, *Leelanau County, Michigan - Land of Delight Vacation Guide 1961;* **192** postcard, Lynn Contos; map, *Vacation at Northport and Leelanau Township,* circa 1945; **193** top ad, *Leelanau Enterprise,* July 2, 1953; bottom ad, *Leelanau Enterprise,* August 16, 1934; **194** top ad, *Leelanau Enterprise,* July 19, 1928; bottom ad, *Leelanau Enterprise,* August 16,

1928; bottom postcard, Lynn Contos; **196** middle postcard, Lynn Contos; ad, *West Michigan, Playground of a Nation,* 1938; **197** postcards, Lynn Contos; ad, *Northport Tribune,* August 4, 1949; **198** ad, *Leelanau County, Michigan - Land of Delight Vacation Guide 1961;* **199** ad, *Vacation Handbook and Fisherman's Guide Leelanau County,* 1938; postcards, Lynn Contos; **200** bottom postcard, Lynn Contos; **201** air mail envelope, Lynn Contos; **202** top, Lynn Contos; bottom, Jill Cheney; **204** ad, *Vacation Handbook and Fisherman's Guide Leelanau County,* 1938; **205** ad, *Vacation Handbook and Fisherman's Guide Leelanau County,* 1942; top postcard, Northport Area Heritage group; bottom photo, Grand Rapids Public Library; **206** bottom postcard, Leelanau Historical Society; **208** bottom, Lynn Contos; **211** top right, Lynn Contos; bottom right, Jill Cheney; *Cedar Lodge, Northport Point, Michigan - at the Top of Grand Traverse Bay,* circa 1950; **212** top photo, Omena Historical Society; bottom photo, Leelanau Historical Society; ad, adapted from a 1927 ad by Rob Burdick; **214** Omena Historical Society; **215** top, Leelanau Historical Society; **216** ad, *Leelanau Enterprise,* July 28, 1928; bottom right, Omena Historical Society; **217** top photo, Omena Historical Society; ad, *Leelanau County, Michigan - Land of Delight Vacation Guide 1961;* **218** ad adapted from 1926 ad by Rob Burdick; **219** postcard, Jill Cheney; ad, adapted from 1935 ad by Rob Burdick; **220** ad, *Vacation Handbook and Fisherman's Guide Leelanau County,* 1942; bottom, Jill Cheney; **221** ad, *Leelanau Enterprise,* July 10, 1930; bottom, Jill Cheney; **222** bottom, Omena Historical Society; **223** ad, *Vacation and Fisherman's Guide Leelanau County,* 1938; bottom, Omena Historical Society; **224** ad, *Vacation Days in the Grand Traverse Bay Region,* 1946; postcard, Leelanau Historical Society; **225** left postcard, Jill Cheney; top photo, Leelanau Historical Society; **226** top, Leelanau Historical Society; bottom, *Leelanau, Little Finger of Michigan,* circa 1943; **227** Leelanau Historical Society; **228** ad, *Visitor's Guide - West Michigan Vacation Directory,* c 1933; **229** ad, *Carefree Days in West Michigan,* 1950; **230** ad, Leelanau Historical Society; bottom, Jill Cheney; **231** ad, *Leelanau Enterprise,* July 11, 1929; right postcard, Karl Bahle/Owen Bahle Collection; **236** photos, Leelanau Historical Society; **238** bottom, Phil Balyeat; **239** Phil Balyeat; **241** Phil Balyeat; **247** MDOT.

All other postcards, photos, and ephemera are from the authors' collection. For organizations, we used the name that was contemporary to the time of the illustration. Vintage Views Press will be happy to rectify any credit omissions or inaccuracies in future editions.

Bibliography & Sources Cited

Sources cited in the text are asterisked. Dates in brackets are approximate.

Books, Pamphlets, Brochures, Maps, and Serials:

At Frankfort Michigan:Enjoy Island Comfort, Inland Conveniences. Frankfort, Mich.: Frankfort Chamber of Commerce, [1940-1950].

*Auto Ferry Across Lake Michigan Via Ann Arbor Railroad. [N.p.: Ann Arbor Railroad], 1932.

Barnes, Al. *Let's Fly Backwards.* Detroit, MI.: Harlo Press, 1976.

---------. *Vinegar Pie and Other Tales of the Grand Traverse Region.* Detroit, MI.: Wayne State University Press, 1959.

Barnett, LeRoy. *A Drive Down Memory Lane: The Named State and Federal Highways of Michigan.* Allegan Forest, Mich.: Priscilla Press, 2004.

*Beautiful Leelanau County - Home of the Sleeping Bear Dunes. [Suttons Bay, Mich.: Leelanau County Chamber of Commerce, 1965].

Benzie Area Historical Society. *Shared Moments: A Journey in Time.* Gaithersburg, Maryland: Signature Book Printing, [2007].

Benzie County Fishing and Vacation Guide. Beulah, Mich.: Andrew Jackson and W.O. Kiracofe, 1937-1941.

*Benzie County Vacationland. N.p.: n.p., [1950-1955].

Bevier, Thomas. *Images of Benzie County.* Virginia Beach, Virginia: Donning Company Publishers, 1998.

Blacklock, Allen B. *Blacklock's History of Elberta.* Manistee, Mich.: West Graf/J.B. Publications, 1975.

A Brief History of Leelanau County. Leland, Mich.: Leelanau County Clerks Office, 1964.

*Camp Caho. N.p.; [Camp Caho, 1925].

*Camp Delight - In the Heart of Vacationland. N.p.: [Camp Delight, 1924].

*Camp Tosebo. N.p.: [Camp Tosebo, 1965].

Case, Leonard. *Benzie County; A Bicentennial Reader.* N.p.: Benzie County Bi-Centennial Commission, [1976].

---------.*Crystal Gazer.* [Benzonia]: Benzie Area Historical Society, [1985].

Cedar Lodge, Northport Point, Michigan - at the Top of Grand Traverse Bay. [Northport, Mich.: Cedar Lodge, 1950].

*Chimney Corners - Crystal Lake North Shore. N.p.: [Chimney Corners, 1940].

Cockrell, Ron. *D.H. Day's Kingdom: A Special History Study of Glen Haven Village Historic District, Sleeping Bear Dunes National Lakeshore, Michigan.* Omaha, Nebraska: National Park Service Midwest Regional Office, [1984].

Congregational Summer Assembly, *In 1948 Vacation with Us.* N.p.: n.p., 1948.

---------. *In 1947 Vacation with Us.* N.p.: n.p., 1947.

Crystal Beach Resort, Formerly Known as Pautz Resort. N.p.: [Crystal Beach Resort, 1940].

*The Crystal Lake and Platte Lakes Region. N.p.: n.p., [1925].

*Crystalaire Camp for Girls. N.p., n.p. [1950].

Day, D.H. (Henry David). *Glen Lake Region.* Traverse City: Herald and Record Co., 1911.

Day Forest Estates on Beautiful Glen Lake. N.p.: [Day Forest Estates, 1928].

D.H. Day State Park/Benzie Unit. [Lansing, Mich.: Michigan Department of Conservation, 1960].

Dickinson, Julia Terry. *The Story of Leelanau.* Omena: Solle's Bookshop, 1951.

Elberta, Home of the Ann Arbor Carferries. N.p.: Elberta Chamber of Commerce, [1950].

Empire Area Heritage Group. *Some Other Day (Remembering Empire).* Empire, Mich.: Empire Area Heritage Group, 1987.

---------. *Remembering Empire Through Pictures.* Empire, Mich.: Empire Area Heritage Group, 2012.

*Follow the M-22 Portion of the Michigamee Trail - Main Line to Sleeping Bear Dune. N.p.: [M-22 Association of the Michigamee Trail, 1966].

*Glenwood Resort, Onekama, Michigan on Portage Lake. N.p.: [Glenwood Resort, 1930].

God's Country and Your Vacation - Manistee County, Michigan. N.p., n.p., [1940].

*Grand Traverse Bay Region: Michigan's Sunshine Corner. Traverse City, Mich.: Traverse City Chamber of Commerce, 1944.

Grand Traverse Region. N.p.: Automobile Club of Michigan, 1939.

Grand Traverse Bay Region by the Old AAA Traveler. N.p.: Automobile Club of Michigan, 1939.

*Grand Traverse, The Summer Land. [Traverse City, Mich.: Traverse City Board of Trade, 1915].

Harmony Camp Tourist Cottages and Cabins. [Onekama, Mich.: Harmony Camp, 1930].

History of Arcadia. [Arcadia, Mich.]: Arcadia Township Historical Commission, 1993.

History of Leelanau Township/ By the Leelanau Township Historical Writers Group. [Leland, Mich.]: Friends of the Leelanau Township Library, 1982.

Holmes, Amanda J. Omena, A Place in Time: A Sesquicentennial History 1852-2002. Omena, Mich.: Omena Historical Society, 2003.

Huey, Michael. Straight as the Pine, Sturdy as the Oak: Skipper & Cora Beals and Major & Helen Huey in the Early Years of Camp Leelanau for Boys, the Leelanau Schools, and the Homestead in Glen Arbor. Volume one: 1921-1963. Vienna, Austria: Schlebrugge.Editor, 2013.

Johnson, Charles. A History of Old Settlements from Leelanau County. [Grand Rapids, Mich.: Charles Johnson, 1995].

Kalt, Brian C. Sixties Sandstorm: The Fight Over the Establishment of a Sleeping Bear Dunes National Lakeshore, 1961-1970. East Lansing. Mich.: Michigan State University Press, 2001.

Kelly, Kerry. Glen Haven Village. Traverse City, Mich.: Friends of Sleeping Bear Dunes, 2007.

---------. Lighthouses. Traverse City, Mich.: Friends of Sleeping Bear Dunes, 2007.

---------. U.S. Life-Saving Service. Traverse City, Mich.: Friends of Sleeping Bear Dunes, 2011.

King's Official Guide. Section Seven. Automobile Routes of Michigan and Northern Indiana. Chicago: S. J.King, 1916-1918.

Karamanski, Theodore J. A Nationalized Lakeshore: The Creation and Administration of Sleeping Bear Dunes National Lakeshore. Omaha, Nebraska.: U.S. Department of the Interior, National Park Service, 2000.

Korn, Claire V. Michigan State Parks: Yesterday Through Tomorrow. East Lansing. Mich.: Michigan State University Press, 1989.

Leelanau County Board of Supervisors. Leelanau - The Little Finger of Michigan. Empire, Mich.: The Studio on Glen Lake, [1943].

*Leelanau County Michigan, Land of Delight Vacation Guide 1961. N.p., n.p. 1961.

*Leelanau Enterprise, Road Map and Business Directory of Leelanau County. Leland, Mich.: Leelanau Enterprise, [1925].

---------.Vacation Handbook and Fisherman's Guide, Leelanau County. Leland, Mich.: Leelanau Enterprise, 1938-1942.

Leelanau For Boys. [Glen Arbor, Mich.: Leelanau Schools, 1950].

*Leelanau Homestead: A Unit of the Leelanau Schools. [Glen Arbor, Mich.: The Leelanau Homestead, 1957].

*Leelanau in Color. [Glen Arbor, Michigan: The Leelanau Schools, 1950].

*Leelanau Lodge on Delightful Lake Leelanau. [Lake Leelanau, Mich.: Leelanau Lodge,1950].

Leelanau Scenic Heritage Route. [Traverse City]: Northwest Michigan Council of Governments, [2005].

Leland Golf and Yacht Club. Resort Directory of Leland and Surrounding Region. Leland, Mich.: Leelanau Enterprise, 1937.

*Leland Lodge - Your Summer Way of Life. [Leland, Mich.: Leland Lodge, 1950].

Littell, Edmund M. 100 Years in Leelanau. Leland, Mich.: The Print Shop, 1965.

*Little Eden Camp, Onekama, Michigan. N.p.: [Little Eden Camp, 1930].

Lund, Orpha. A History of Lund's Scenic Garden. N.p.: n.p., [1965].

*Lunds Scenic Garden. [Maple City, Mich., Mr. and Mrs. E.K. Lund, 1950].

M-22 Scenic Corridor: Preserving Our View from the Road. Leland, Mich.: Leelanau Conservancy, [2002].

*M-22 "The Manitou Trail." Frankfort, Mich.: M-22 Association. [1955].

Manistee & Northeastern Railroad. Summer Resorts, Fisherman's Guide, Train Service, June 1912. N.p.: [Manistee & Northeastern Railroad, 1912].

*Manistee County, Michigan. [Manistee, Mich.: Manistee Board of Commerce], 1952.

Manistee County Offer You Carefree Summer Days. N.p.:Manistee Board of Commerce, [1940].

*Manistee, Michigan on the Scenic Paved Highway M-11 - US-31 in the Heart of Vacationland. Manistee, Mich.: American Printing Co., [1930].

Manistee-Portage Region: Arcadia, Onekama, Bear Lake. Manistee, Mich.: American Printing Co., [1930].

*Manistee Vacation Guide, 1939 Edition. Manistee Mich.: Examiner Printing Co., 1939.

*McCracken, Lawrence. McCraken's 1940 Guide to Michigan. Pontiac, Mich.: Lawrence McCracken, 1940.

Michigan Department of State Highways. History of Michigan Highways and the Michigan Department of State Highways. Lansing, Mich.: Michigan Dept. of State Highways, 1966.

*Michigan: A Guide to the Wolverine State. New York, N.Y.: Oxford University Press, 1941.

*Michigan Scenic Highways: Around Lake Michigan Tour. Lansing, Mich.: Magazine of Michigan, 1933.

*Michigan Tourist and Resort Association. *Visitor's Guide of West Michigan Vacation Directory*, [N.p., Michigan Tourist and Resort Association,1933].

*---------. *West Michigan Vacation Directory*. Grand Rapids, Mich.: Michigan Tourist and Resort Association 1924-1933.

Michigan State Highway Commission, *Biennial Report of the State Highway Commissioner*. [Lansing, Mich.]: Michigan State Highway Department, 1913-1959.

Michigan's Scenic Highways: Around Lake Michigan Tour. Lansing, Mich.: Magazine of Michigan, 1933.

Miller, Frank W. *Camp Arcadia: The First Sixty Years*. [Manistee, Mich.: F. W. Miller, 1982].

More Than a Century: Suttons Bay, Michigan, 1976 Bicentennial Handbook. Suttons Bay: Suttons Bay Chamber of Commerce, [1976].

Morrison, Roger Leroy. *The History and Development of Michigan Highways*. Ann Arbor, Mich.; University of Michigan, 1938.

Nelson's Mackinaw Trolling Camp. Zeeland, Mich.: Abe, the Printer, [1944].

Northport Centennial: 100 Years: 1949-1949. Northport, Mich.: Chamber of Commerce, 1949.

O-Nek-A-Ma: Place of Great Beauty. [Onekama: Onekama Resort Association, [1930].

Official Automobile Blue Book. Chicago: Automobile Blue Books, Inc. 1914-1929.

Old Orchard Inn - Tonawatha- On Glen Lake, Michigan. N.p.: Old Orchard Inn, [1954].

Park Hotel - Frankfort, Michigan. [Frankfort, Mich.:Park Hotel, 1940].

Parks of the People. [Lansing, Mich.]: Department of Conservation, [1924].

Peters, Erhardt. *Loving Leland*. Ludington, Mich.: Black Creek Press, 2004.

Phelps, William Henry. *Ye Lakes and Hills of Michigan*. Detroit, Mich.: Michigan Christian Advocate Press, [1933].

Pinebrook for Girls: A Country Boarding School. [Glen Arbor, Mich.: Leelanau Schools, 1950].

Portage Point Inn- "Among Michigan's Finest." Onekama, Mich.: Portage Point Inn, [1935].

A Proposed Sleeping Bear National Seashore, Natural History Report. [N.p.]: U.S. Department of the Interior, National Park Service, 1961.

Rader, Robert Dwight. *Beautiful Glen Arbor Township*. Glen Arbor, Mich.: Glen Arbor History Group, 1977.

Raff's Mackinaw Trolling Camp. [Northport, Mich.: Raff's Mackinaw Trolling Camp, 1935].

Robbins, Sabin. *A Hundred Summers: An Affectionate History of Northport Point*. Elk Rapids, Mich.: Bayshore Books, [1999].

Rogers, Frank Foster. *History of the Michigan State Highway Department, 1905-1933*. Lansing, Mich.: [Franklin DeKleine Company], 1933.

Sandman, Jeffrey P. and Sandman, Peter R. *Soaring and Gliding: The Sleeping Bear Dunes National Lakeshore Area*. Charleston, South Carolina: Arcadia Publishing, 2006.

Sandman, Pete. *The Landmarks of Frankfort, Michigan*. [Frankfort, Mich.: P. Sandman, 1987].

---------. *Views from God's Country*. Frankfort, Mich.: Benzie County Record Patriot, 1981].

Scarborough's Official Tour Book. Indiana, Ohio, Michigan, Wisconsin, and Trunk Lines. Indianapolis: Scarborough Motor Guide Company, 1916-1917.

Sheffer, Richard L. *Peshawbestown*. [Mt. Pleasant, Mich.: Central Michigan University, 1970].

Siepker, Barbara. *Historic Cottages of Glen Lake*. Glen Arbor, MI.: Leelanau Press, 2008.

Sleeping Bear Area Information Map & Tips About the Proposed National Lakeshore. Ann Arbor, Mich.: Michigan Parks Association, [1963].

Sleeping Bear Dunes Park. [Empire, Mich.: Stocking Land Co., 1968].

Sleeping Bear Dunes Wagon Rides. [Glen Haven, Mich.: Marion and Louis Warnes, 1975].

Sleeping Bear Dunesmobile Scenic Dune Rides. [Glen Haven, Mich.: Marion and Louis Warnes, 1956-1959].

Sommers, Laurie Kay. *Fishtown: Leland, Michigan's Historic Fishery*. Traverse City, Mich.: Arbutus Press, 2012.

Sprenger's Resort Lakeview Hotel. [Onekama, Mich.: Sprenger's Lakeview Hotel, 1930].

*Stace, Arthur William. *Along Michigan Coasts*. Ann Arbor, Mich.: Booth Newspapers, 1937.

*---------. *Michigan's Mystic Dunes*. Ann Arbor, Mich.: Booth Newspapers, 1939.

Stern, Jane and Michael. *Amazing America*. New York: Random House, [1978].

Stonehouse, Frederick. *Wreck Ashore: The United State Life-Saving Service of the Great Lakes*. Duluth: Lake Superior Port Cities, Inc., 1994.

Suttons Bay, Leelanau County, Michigan. [Suttons Bay, Mich.: Suttons Bay Chamber of Commerce], 1954.

Tourist Guide of the West Michigan Pike. [Muskegon, Mich.: West Michigan Pike Association], 1922.

Vacation at Northport and Leelanau Township: The Tip of the Little Finger of Michigan. [Northport, Mich.: n.p., 1945].

Vacation Days in Michigan's Grand Traverse Bay Region. [Traverse City, Mi.: Traverse City Area Chamber of Commerce, 1953-1963].

Vacation Days in the Grand Traverse Bay Region. [Traverse City, Mi.: Traverse City Area Chamber of Commerce, 1946-1952].

 Vacation Guide Manistee, Mich. Manistee.Mich.: Examiner Printing Co., 1945-1946.

Wakefield, Lawrence. *Leelanau County Postcard History*. [Leland, Mich.]: Leelanau County Historical Society, [1992].

Watervale Inn and Cottages, Watervale, Mich. N.p.: [Watervale Inn, 1925].

Watervale: The Diamond Years 1917-1992. N.p.: [Watervale, 1993].

Weeks, George. *Mem-Ka-Weh: Dawning of the Grand Traverse Band of Ottawa and Chippewa Indians*. [N.p.]: Grand Traverse Band of Ottawa and Chippewa Indians, 1992.

---------. *Sleeping Bear: Its Lore, Legends and First People*. Glen Arbor, Mich.: Cottage Book Shop and the Historical Society of Michigan, [1988].

---------. *Sleeping Bear: Yesterday and Tomorrow*. [N.P.]: University of Michigan Press and Petoskey Publishing Company, 1990, 2005.

West Michigan Pike Association, *Maps, Routes and Tourist's Directory of the West Michigan Pike*. Muskegon, Mich., Dana Press, 1914.

*West Michigan Tourist and Resort Association, *Carefree Days in West Michigan*. Grand Rapids, Mich.: West Michigan Tourist and Resort Association, 1939-1960.

*---------. *Preview of Your Complete Vacation in West Michigan*. Grand Rapids, Mich.: West Michigan Tourist and Resort Association 1937.

*---------. *West Michigan, Playground of a Nation*. Grand Rapids, Mich.: West Michigan Tourist and Resort Association 1938.

*---------. *Winter Sports in West Michigan*. Grand Rapids, Mich.: West Michigan Tourist and Resort Association, 1954-1956.

*West Michigan Tourist Association. *Carefree Days in West Michigan*. Grand Rapids, Mich.: West Michigan Tourist Association, 1961-1969.

---------. *Lake Michigan Circle Tour*. Grand Rapids, Mich.: West Michigan Tourist Association, 1988-1989.

Yock, Dr. Louis for the Benzie Area Historical Society. *Lost Benzie County*. Charlestown, South Carolina: Arcadia Publishing, 2011.

---------. *Crystal Lake*. Charlestown, South Carolina: Arcadia Publishing, 2009.

Newspapers:
Detroit News. 1948.
Emmet County Graphic, 1938.
Glen Arbor Sun, 2000-2014.
Grand Rapids Herald, 1913-1940.
Grand Rapids Press, 1913-1950.
Leelanau Enterprise and Tribune, 1913-1955.
Northport Leader, 1925-26.
Northport Tribune, 1947-1949.
Suttons Bay Courier 1949.
Traverse City Record Eagle, 1913-1955.

Periodicals:
Ford Times, April 1948.
Good Year News, October 1940.
Grand Rapids Progress, August 1915.
Michigan Magazine, May 1929.
Motor News, June 1955.
National Geographic Magazine, April 1934.
Northern Michigan Magazine, February 1928.

Special Collections:
Archives of Michigan, Michigan Historical Center
Bentley Historical Library, University of Michigan
Grand Rapids History & Special Collections,
          Grand Rapids Public Library

ENDS

About the Authors

M. Christine Byron & Thomas R. Wilson

Christine and Tom share a love of northern Michigan and a fascination with its history. They are especially interested in the history of Michigan's tourism industry. Their collection of antique postcards and tourist and travel ephemera was the inspiration for their five books: *Vintage Views Along Scenic M-22 including Sleeping Bear Dunes* (2015); *Vintage Views Along the West Michigan Pike* (2011); *Vintage Views of the Mackinac Straits Region* (2007); *Vintage Views of the Charlevoix – Petoskey Region (2005); and Vintage Views of Leelanau County* (2002). Three of their books have won Michigan Notable Book awards from the Library of Michigan. Their book on the West Michigan Pike won a 2012 State History Award from the Historical Society of Michigan.

Christine Byron is retired from her position of 15 years as the Local Historical Collections librarian for the Grand Rapids Public Library. Previously she had been a bookseller for 22 years, working in several bookstores in Grand Rapids, and later as a district manager for an independent bookstore chain. Christine has an undergraduate degree from Aquinas Collage and a Masters in Library Science from Western Michigan University. She is an avid reader of Michigan history and has collected old Michigan travel and tourist memorabilia for over 25 years.

Tom Wilson is retired from Sears Roebuck and Company, where he held various positions in his 38 year career, including technical manager for Sears Home Services. Tom attended Grand Valley State University and is a life-long student of history. He is an avid postcard collector and has collected Michigan real photo postcards for over 25 years. Tom operates a business creating prints from old Michigan and Great Lakes tourist and travel ephemera.

The authors are active members of the West Michigan Postcard Club. They are also members of the several local historical societies including the Grand Rapids Historical Society, the Leelanau Historical Society, the Historical Society of Michigan and Friends of Michigan History. Tom serves on the board of the Grand Rapids Historical Commission. Christine and Tom are married and live in a 1912 Arts and Crafts bungalow in Grand Rapids. They love spending as much time as possible touring Michigan's scenic roads.